An Introduction to Green Homes

Readers of this text may be interested in the following publications from the Appraisal Institute:

- *The Appraisal of Real Estate*, 13th edition
- *Appraising the Appraisal: The Art of Appraisal Review*, 2nd edition
- *Appraising Residential Properties*, 4th edition
- *The Dictionary of Real Estate Appraisal*, 5th edition
- *Scope of Work*, now available in print or as an audio book

Appraisal Institute®

Professionals Providing Real Estate Solutions

An Introduction to Green Homes

by Alan F. Simmons, SRPA, LEED AP

Appraisal Institute • 550 West Van Buren • Chicago, IL 60607 • www.appraisalinstitute.org

The Appraisal Institute advances global standards, methodologies, and practices through the professional development of property economics worldwide.

Reviewers:	Sandra K. Adomatis, SRA
	Thomas A. Dorsey, MAI, SRA
	Diane M. Gilbert, MAI, SRA
	Jason La Fleur, LEED AP
Chief Executive Officer:	Frederick H. Grubbe
Director, Marketing & Member Resources:	Hope Atuel
Senior Manager, Publications:	Stephanie Shea-Joyce
Senior Technical Writer:	Michael McKinley
Technical Book Editor:	Emily Ruzich
Manager, Book Design/Production:	Michael Landis

This book is printed on paper stock that is 30% post-consumer waste.

Library of Congress Cataloging-in-Publication Data

Simmons, Alan F., 1939-
An introduction to green homes / by Alan F. Simmons.
p. cm.
ISBN 978-1-935328-09-4
1. Real property--Valuation--United States. 2. Ecological houses--Valuation--United States.
3. Sustainable buildings--Design and construction--Standards--United States. I. Title.
HD1389.5.U6.S56 2010
333.33'82--dc22

2010013187

Table of Contents

About the Author

Alan F. Simmons, SRPA, LEED AP, CDEI, was a REALTOR® for 12 years and an appraiser for more than 30 years. He is now a real estate education specialist working full time in teaching and course development. Mr. Simmons spent most of his life and working career in the state of New York but now lives in Colorado Springs. He has a BA in economics from Union College and has taught in 43 states. Mr. Simmons has taught primarily for appraisal organizations, but he has also instructed for REALTOR® and assessor organizations as well as private schools.

Mr. Simmons has been the developer of Appraisal Institute courses on appraisal principles and procedures as well as eight online seminars on topics including residential and commercial green building. He has also developed and taught Appraisal Institute classroom courses on topics such as the Uniform Residential Appraisal Report form, Federal Housing Administration appraisals, appraising condominiums, and residential green building. He has authored various articles and publications.

Mr. Simmons has served in leadership positions in REALTOR® and appraisal organizations and received the 1994 Ellwood Award as "Appraiser of the Year" in the state of New York. He has served the Appraisal Institute as a chapter president and regional representative. Mr. Simmons received the 1992 George L. Schmutz Memorial Award from the Appraisal Institute for contributions to the advancement of appraisal knowledge and best technical writing. He is also a Certified Distance Education Instructor (CDEI) and a LEED Accredited Professional (AP) through the U.S. Green Building Council.

Foreword

Green building is one of the fastest-growing movements in the housing industry today. More than just a passing trend, the green building movement is a response to the pressing environmental problems prevalent in our society and provides tangible environmental, community, and economic benefits, improving health and public spaces and lowering building and energy costs.

An Introduction to Green Homes provides the appraiser with an overview of programs, organizations, and products that relate to environmentally responsible building and remodeling. Green home and product certification programs like LEED and Energy Star are described, as are popular green home products and features such as energy-efficient appliances, toxin-free flooring and insulation materials, and vegetated roofs. This guide also provides appraisers with an overview of environmental organizations that are leading the way in green building, including the U.S. Green Building Council and NAHB Green, and directs them to a variety of online resources where the most up-to-date information is available. Case studies focusing on various attributes of green homes are provided. The text concludes with a thorough discussion of how green features affect the valuation of homes.

Green homes present new opportunities to residential appraisers. As the presence of green homes increases in the housing market, appraisers who are knowledgeable in all things green can gain an edge on the competition. *An Introduction to Green Homes* provides a solid foundation for residential appraisers to diversify their practices and become knowledgeable about one of most important forces influencing today's housing market.

Leslie P. Sellers, MAI, SRA
2010 President, Appraisal Institute

Preface

Green building is a hot topic that is being discussed in all segments of society. It is difficult to pick up a newspaper or magazine or turn on the TV without hearing about some topic associated with green building, such as global warming, dwindling water supplies, the ozone layer, the oil crisis, greenhouse gases, carbon cap and trade policies, or renewable energy resources.

Green building programs for residential properties, such as Energy Star, have been around in various forms for the past 15 years. Also, more than 200 local and regional green residential building programs are active, primarily through the National Association of Home Builders (NAHB). Leadership in Energy and Environmental Design (LEED) is a program of the U. S. Green Building Council (USGBC) and the most recognized program in commercial green buildings. In 2008, the USGBC released a new rating program known as LEED for Homes as well as guidelines for the remodeling and renovation of existing residences known as REGREEN. Finally, in 2010 the Council of Multiple Listing Services, the Multi-Regional Multiple Listing Service, the National Association of Realtors, the Appraisal Institute, and other organizations created The Green Multiple Listing Service Tool Kit, which provides guidance for local multiple listing services that wish to implement green initiatives. We will look at the impact and market acceptance of these and other similar programs throughout this book.

This book also provides an introduction to green building practices and a review of how these practices impact value. Various green building products and available government incentives are discussed throughout the text.

Real estate appraisers are finding themselves in a dynamic market right now and are likely just seeing the tip of the iceberg. Green building has the potential to have a huge impact on the housing market and the economy in the coming years. It is no longer just a fad, but has matured into a multibillion-dollar industry. Appraisers need to strive to keep up with the changes.

CHAPTER 1

Green Building Overview

Introduction

The green building movement is gaining momentum and creating significant changes in the way houses are built as well as the way people live. According to the U.S. Green Building Council, www.usgbc.org, green building has flourished despite the economic downturn of 2008 and 2009, and sales generated by environmentally friendly home building are projected to increase.

Residential green building is geographically dispersed. While some areas have seen little in the way of new residential green construction, this type of construction accounts for close to 25% of the market in areas such as Denver and Seattle.

Appraising any type of building that is different presents challenges. Green buildings incorporate different designs, site planning, building materials, and mechanical systems. Appraisers need to become competent in analyzing and evaluating these new features; this often requires more extensive market research.

Green building is not a "flash in the pan;" it is here to stay, and the practice enjoys an increasing amount of popular support among a growing number of people who recognize the advantages and support the objectives of sustainable development practices. Green building has extensive governmental support, as evidenced in mandates and financial incentives.

Green building appraisals can present opportunities for residential appraisers. Green buildings will become an increasing share of residential appraisals. Those who become knowledgeable and proficient in appraising these types of properties may be able to gain in their market share of appraisal business.

Green building is an opportunity for appraisers to diversify their practices and develop work as appraisal consultants. They may become known as specialists in green building through specialized study or gaining a certification. Appraisers can provide consulting services to builders, developers, or even property owners on proposed green construction or renovations.

Definitions

Unfortunately, no universally accepted definition of *green building* exists yet. The U.S. Green Building Council (USGBC), a nonprofit organization dedicated to expanding sustainable building practices, defines a *green building* as a building that is designed, constructed, and operated to boost environmental, economic, health, and productivity performance over that of conventional buildings.[1] The National Association of Home Builders' National Green Building Program, www.nahbgreen.org, defines a *green home* as one that pays attention to energy efficiency, water and resource conservation, the use of sustainable or recycled products, and measures to protect indoor air quality. The Office of the Federal Environmental Executive (OFEE) defines *green building* as "the practice of 1) increasing the efficiency with which buildings and their sites use energy, water, and materials, and 2) reducing building impacts on human health and the environment, through better siting, design, construction, operation, maintenance, and removal–the complete building life cycle."[2] Finally, the *Dictionary of Real Estate Appraisal*, fifth edition, defines *green building* as "the practice of creating structures and using processes that are environmentally responsible and resource-efficient throughout a building's lifecycle from siting to design, construction, operation, maintenance, renovation, and deconstruction; also known as *sustainable* or *high-performance building*."

Some common themes can be found in these definitions:

- The environment
- Energy efficiency
- Resource conservation
- Indoor air quality and health benefits
- Sustainability

---

1. USGBC, *Building Momentum: National Trends and Prospects for High-Performance Green Buildings* (Washington, D.C.: USGBC, 2003). (Based on the April 2002 Green Building Roundtable and prepared for the U.S. Senate Committee on Environment and Public Works.) Available at www.usgbc.org. Direct link: http://www.usgbc.org/Docs/Resources/043003_hpgb_whitepaper.pdf/.
2. OFEE, *The Federal Commitment to Green Building: Experiences and Expectations* (2003). For more information, visit http://ofee.gov/.

The internationally recognized definition of *sustainability* was produced by the World Commission on Environment and Development (WCED) in a 1987 report. The report defined *sustainable development* as "development that meets the needs of the present without compromising the ability of future generations to meet their own needs."[3] The architectural and design communities have embraced this definition as a substantial component of their thinking via the use of innovative sustainable design elements, practices, and products.

In regard to buildings, the word *green* is often used interchangeably with the word *sustainable*. Some people think that the term *high-performance* better describes the combination of features that allow a building to operate more efficiently while consuming fewer resources. It is important to understand the distinctions as to what makes a building green. The term *green* is often thrown around indiscriminately. People hear and see ads that tout "green" cars and appliances. In fact, *green* was the most trademarked term in 2007; this is akin to the past trend of labeling food products as "natural" or "all natural," even though it was not made clear what those terms actually meant. Today, some builders like to incorporate only a few green features in a building and then proudly proclaim it to be "green."

Why Is Green Building Important?

According to the USGBC, buildings in the United States account for approximately 37% of the country's energy use and 68% of the country's electricity use. Buildings in the United States also consume 12% of the country's fresh water supplies, 88% of the country's potable water supplies (i.e., water that is fit for human consumption), and 40% of the country's raw materials. These buildings collectively generate about 30% of the municipal solid waste streams, 36% of total emissions of carbon dioxide, the primary greenhouse gas associated with global climate change, and 46% of sulfur dioxide emissions, a precursor to acidic deposition. This creates a tremendous drain on the earth's natural resources, which in turn has a huge impact on the economy. Any efficiency that can be gained in building construction, operations, and maintenance will have a beneficial impact on the future.

Buildings have a profound impact on the natural environment, health, the economy, and productivity. The U.S. Environmental Protection Agency (EPA) classifies indoor air quality as one of the top five environmental health risks affecting the health and performance

3. WCED, *Our Common Future* (Oxford: Oxford University Press, 1987), 43. Note that the WCED is also known as the Brundtland Commission and this report is also known as the Brundtland Report.

of occupants today. New research points to links between green buildings and labor productivity–a business expense that dwarfs other building operating expenses.[4]

According to Rick Fedrizzi, President of the USGBC, "Green building can stimulate the economy at a level one and a half times larger than the federal stimulus bill. In terms of climate change, a commitment to energy efficiency would be the equivalent to taking more than 200 million vehicles off the road." A report released in July 2009 by McKinsey & Company stated that investing in the energy efficiency of buildings and other non-transportation sectors could reduce the nation's energy consumption by 23% by the year 2020, save the U.S. economy $1.2 trillion, and reduce greenhouse gas emissions by 1.1 gigatons annually. The report calls for a national plan guided by five principles:

1. Recognize energy efficiency as an important resource that can help meet future energy needs.
2. Formulate and launch an integrated portfolio of proven and piloted approaches.
3. Identify methods for providing funding.
4. Forge alignment among utilities, regulators, government agencies, manufacturers, and energy consumers.
5. Foster innovation in the development and use of next-generation energy-efficiency technologies.[5]

The 2008 book *Hot, Flat, and Crowded: Why We Need a Green Revolution–and How It Can Renew America* discusses how global warming, the stunning rise of middle classes all over the world, and rapid population growth have made the planet dangerously unstable. In this book, David Rothkopf, an energy expert and visiting scholar at the Carnegie Endowment, states that we as a nation have

> ...reinvented ourselves as a continental industrial power in the nineteenth century, as a global industrial power in the twentieth century, and then as a global information society in the twenty-first century. Now we have to–for our own sake and the world's–reinvent ourselves one more time. Making America the world's greenest country is not a selfless act of charity or naïve moral indulgence. It is now a core national security and economic interest.[6]

---

4. USGBC, *Building Momentum*, 3.
5. USGBC, "Green building is a crucial and urgent economic and environmental imperative, says new McKinsey report" (July 29, 2009 press release). Available online at www.usgbc.org. Direct link: http://www.usgbc.org/News/PressReleaseArchive.aspx/.
6. Thomas L. Friedman, *Hot, Flat, and Crowded* (New York: Farrar, Straus & Giroux, 2008).

Aspects of Green Building

Green building encompasses water efficiency, electricity efficiency, waste management, and indoor environmental quality.

Water Efficiency

A tremendous amount of water is consumed by buildings in the United States. However, gains are being made in this area. U.S. industries use 36% less water today than they did in 1950, due largely to rigorous water re-use strategies.[7]

The EPA's Energy Policy Act of 1992 mandated the use of water-conserving plumbing fixtures to reduce water use in residential, commercial, and institutional buildings. At that time, the typical toilet flush used three to four gallons of water. Recognizing that water would become an increasingly scarce resource in the future, the Energy Policy Act of 1992 restricted water use from various fixtures as shown in Exhibit 1.1.

Landscape irrigation practices also consume large quantities of potable water. Outdoor uses, primarily landscaping, account for 30% of the 26 billion gallons of water that are consumed daily in the United States.[8]

While water has always been a concern in regions that receive little annual rainfall, such as the Southwest and mountain states, water efficiency has become a growing concern all over the nation. Since Georgia's severe drought in 2007 and recent dropping water levels in the Great Lakes, water is now seen as an increasingly important resource and commodity impacting areas across the country. Reducing excessive water use while preserving water quality is an important focus of green building.

Exhibit 1.1 Water Use Restrictions (EPA Energy Policy Act of 1992)

Fixture	Flow Requirements
Water closets	1.6 gallons per flush
Urinals	1.0 gallons per flush
Showerheads	2.5 gallons per minute
Faucets	2.5 gallons per minute

Electricity Efficiency

As stated previously in this chapter, buildings in the United Stated account for about 68% of the nation's electricity use. Where does all this electricity go? According to the EPA, the total amount of electricity used by U.S. buildings can be broken down further by building type: residential buildings use 37% of the total electricity used by buildings

7. USGBC, *New Construction & Major Renovation Reference Guide*, Version 2.2, 3rd ed. (October 2007).
8. Ibid.

in the United States, while commercial buildings use 35% and industrial buildings use 28%.

It is surprising to see that residential buildings consume more electricity than commercial or industrial buildings, but the reason is simply that more residential buildings exist than commercial or industrial. As a result, anything that can be done to reduce the use of electricity in homes is a critical issue. Some specific solutions will be discussed later in this book.

The way in which electricity is generated has a huge impact on the environment. Electricity generated from oil and coal impacts the environment in many negative ways, starting with the extraction, transportation, refining, and distribution of these fossil fuels. Coal is rinsed with water, which results in billions of gallons of sludge stored in ponds. Conventional fossil-based generation of electricity releases carbon dioxide, which contributes to global climate change. Coal-fired electric utilities emit almost one-third of the country's nitrogen oxide, a key element in smog, and two-thirds of the country's sulfur dioxide, a key element in acid rain.[9]

Exhibit 1.2 provides a breakdown of how electricity was generated in the United States in 2007 and demonstrates America's reliance on fossil fuels. Adding up the percentages for coal, natural gas, and petroleum shows that 70.6% of American electrical energy needs were met by burning fossil fuels in 2007.

According to the National Renewable Energy Laboratory, www.nrel.gov, fossil fuels are *nonrenewable*, meaning that they draw from finite resources that will eventually dwindle and become too expensive or environmentally damaging to retrieve. On the other hand, *renewable* energy resources–such as wind and solar energy–are constantly replenished and will never run out. Renewable energy sources include wind, solar, geothermal, biomass, hydropower, wave, and tidal sources. In spite of all the recent publicity concerning renewable energy sources, the United States currently gets only 2.4% of its electricity from renewable sources (other than hydropower). Of that 2.4%, 57% comes

Exhibit 1.2 Generation of Electricity in the United States in 2007

Energy Source	Percentage of Total Electricity Generated
Coal	49.1%
Natural gas	20.0%
Nuclear	19.5%
Hydropower	7.1%
Renewable resources	2.4%
Petroleum	1.5%

Based on information from the National Renewable Energy Laboratory, www.nrel.gov.

9. Ibid.

from biomass materials (such as wood), 27% comes from wind, 15% is geothermal, and about 0.5% is solar.

The Obama administration has focused on accelerating the use of renewable energy sources. In his first major presidential speech to the nation before a joint session of Congress in February of 2009, Barack Obama promised to invest $15 billion per year to develop technologies such as wind power, solar power, advanced biofuels, clean coal, and fuel-efficient cars and trucks. The federal government and many states have set goals to obtain 20% of their total energy from renewable sources by the year 2020.

Waste Management

Construction and demolition wastes constitute about 60% of the total nonindustrial waste generated in the United States. In the past, when landfill capacity was readily available and disposal fees were low, recycling or reuse of construction waste was not economically feasible. In recent years, technology has changed and expenses have increased, making the idea of responsible construction waste management more attractive.

Later in this book, some strategies will be discussed that can be adopted to keep construction waste from reaching landfills. Some of these strategies involve new technologies, while others are simply commonsense practices.

Indoor Environmental Quality

Americans spend an average of 90% of their time indoors, where the EPA reports that pollutant levels may run two to five times–and occasionally more than 100 times–higher than outdoor levels.[10] Green building practices can enhance indoor environmental quality and lead to healthier living. Some aspects of indoor environmental quality include

- Exchanging indoor air with filtered outdoor air
- Obtaining optimal indoor air quality
- Creating comfortable living spaces
- Maximizing natural light

Benefits of Green Building

The benefits of green building extend beyond the structure itself. Green building takes a holistic approach. Some of its principles apply to how a site is chosen and developed. Other considerations include the materials that are chosen and how the building systems work together.

---

10. USGBC, *Building Momentum*, 3.

Benefits of green building accrue to the environment itself, the community or society as a whole, and the owners or occupants of the building. Some of these benefits, such as economic benefits, are tangible, while other benefits, such as improved health, are intangible. The following discussion summarizes some of the most important environmental, community, and economic benefits of green building.

Environmental Benefits

Green building can

- Enhance and protect ecosystems
- Improve water quality
- Reduce soil pollution
- Reduce water consumption
- Reduce stormwater runoff
- Reduce solid waste
- Conserve natural resources
- Improve indoor air quality
- Enhance occupant health and comfort
- Reduce heat island effect

Note that the term *heat island effect* refers to the phenomenon of warmer temperatures being experienced in urban landscapes compared to adjacent rural areas as a result of solar energy retention on constructed surfaces. The surfaces of streets, sidewalks, parking lots, and buildings all contribute to this effect. As a result, ambient temperatures in urban areas can be artificially elevated by more than 10° F when compared to surrounding suburban and undeveloped areas. This results in more greenhouse gas and pollution generation as well as increased energy consumption.[11] Reducing the amount of paved surfaces in an area by way of underground parking areas, shade trees, and vegetated roofs can help decrease heat island effects.

Community Benefits

Green building can

- Improve the acoustic environment
- Provide more open space
- Protect natural habitats
- Improve conditions in public areas
- Minimize the strain on infrastructures
- Reduce carbon emissions from transportation
- Improve the overall quality of life

11. Ibid.

Social benefits to the community as a whole are certainly desirable. However, from an appraisal standpoint, the economic advantages of green building are the most relevant.

Economic Benefits

Economic benefits of green building include

- Reduction of operating costs
- Reduction of maintenance costs
- Reduction of reserves for replacement
- Enhancement of asset values
- Improvement of the health of residents
- Optimization of life-cycle economic performance

Economic benefits attributable to green building can be directly measured and employed in valuation analysis. Lower operating costs, reduced maintenance costs, and replacement reserves can certainly result in higher values.

Green Building History

Some elements of green building go back hundreds of years. The Anasazi Indians built their homes in the Southwest region of the United States over a thousand years ago. These dwellings, built underneath overhanging cliffs, were oriented to take advantage of solar heating in the winter and shading in the summer.

The architect Frank Lloyd Wright was a pioneer in residential construction and introduced some startlingly modern ideas between 1900 and 1910, such as long, low, one-story houses, low-pitched roofs with projecting eaves, continuous bands of windows, open interior plans, poured concrete, and concrete block. Wright's philosophy in architecture promoted harmony between the building, its inhabitants, and nature. His homes became part of their surroundings. He minimized his buildings' presence and maximized their practicality. He revolutionized modern architecture with the essentials of ecological design.

However, the high ceilings and expanses of glass commonly found in Wright's residential designs were not energy efficient, nor did he design homes with insulation in mind. This was a common building practice at the time because fossil fuels were cheap and plentiful.

In the 1930s through the 1960s, new technologies such as air conditioning, fluorescent lighting with lower wattage, and structural steel appeared in residential construction. Houses were now routinely insulated with rock wool and fiberglass, but it was not a matter of emphasis.

The early 1970s ushered in the first major energy shortage, which culminated in the oil crisis of 1973 and long lines at gas pumps. The price of home heating oil increased from $0.20 per gallon to $1.00 per gallon in the course of about a year. Just as people began to convert from oil heat to gas heat, the price of gas tripled. Suddenly, it became not only chic but sensible to be energy conscious. Builders and architects started looking at ways to build homes that were more energy efficient.

The main line of attack was to pack in more insulation. In some cases, super-insulated homes led to improper ventilation and moisture problems as houses were built "too tight" for the first time and could not breathe properly. The 1970s also saw the rise in popularity of alternative architecture such as Richard Buckminster Fuller's geodesic dome. Originally invented in 1949, the geodesic dome can attain maximum space related to the environment with minimal use of raw materials.

Builders began to take a broader view in the 1970s. They tried to look at the house as a whole system and figure out better ways to produce houses that are healthier in terms of indoor air quality, more comfortable to live in, and efficient in terms of both energy and cost. Builders were starting to "think green," but it was a slow and uneven process. Few guidelines were in place and research was spotty at best.

A geodesic dome residence

Exhibit 1.3 presents a timeline of significant events in green building history.

Exhibit 1.3 Green Building History Timeline

1970
- The EPA is created by President Richard Nixon for the purpose of protecting human health and safeguarding the natural environment. The first Earth Day is celebrated.

1973
- The American Institute of Architects (AIA) forms an energy task force as a response to the energy crisis.

1977
- The Department of Energy (DOE) is created to address energy conservation.
- The Solar Energy Research Institute (SERI) is formed. (It will become the National Renewable Energy Laboratory in 1991.)

1980
- The Sustainable Buildings Industry Council (SBIC) is founded by the major building trade associations.

1992
- The EPA launches the Energy Star program for consumers to identify energy-efficient products.
- The first local, residential green building program is created in Austin, Texas.

1993
- The USGBC is formed by representatives of the entire building industry.
- President Bill Clinton introduces the "Greening of the White House" Initiative.

1996
- The Built Green Colorado program is introduced to encourage builders to produce homes that are better built and better for the environment

1997
- The Kyoto Protocol sets binding targets for 37 industrialized countries and the European community for reducing greenhouse gas (GHG) emissions.

1998
- The USGBC produces their Leadership in Energy and Environmental Design (LEED) guidelines.

2005
- The Energy Policy Act of 2005 is passed and includes federal building sustainable performance standards.

2007
- President George W. Bush signs Executive Order 13423, which includes federal goals for sustainable design and high-performance buildings.

2009
- The Copenhagen Conference recognizes that climate change is one of the greatest challenges of the present day and actions should be taken to keep any temperature increases to below 2°C. The document is not legally binding.

Based on information from the online article "Green Building Timeline," published by GreenBuilding.com.

CHAPTER 2

Green Building Programs

Energy Star Program

The federal Energy Star program is intended to save money and protect the environment through energy-efficient products and practices. It was introduced by the EPA in 1992 as a voluntary labeling program, intended to reduce greenhouse gas emissions. The first energy-efficient products labeled were computers and monitors. This program was then expanded to include additional office equipment products and residential heating and cooling equipment.[1]

Perhaps most significant to the valuation profession, the EPA partnered with the U.S. Department of Energy in 1996, and today the official Energy Star label can be found on products such as major appliances, lighting fixtures, and home electronics. The Energy Star label has also been extended to cover new homes as well as commercial and industrial buildings.

The program's goal is to partner with private and public sector organizations to deliver information and tools to help people choose energy-efficient practices. The Energy Star program has helped foster more widespread use of technological innovations such as efficient fluorescent lighting, power management systems for office equipment, and low standby energy use. Because of these new technologies, Americans saved an estimated $17 billion in energy expenses during the year 2009. The EPA also partners with organizations around the country in a home retrofit program called Home Performance with Energy Star, in which trained professionals provide homeowners with home energy audits and make recommendations to improve the efficiency and comfort of their homes.

---

1. Much of the information in this section has been gathered from the Energy Star Web site, www.energystar.gov.

The EPA has also made the following estimates:

- Americans have purchased over one billion Energy Star-qualified products.
- More than 100,000 U.S. families live in new homes that have earned the Energy Star rating.
- More than 40% of the American public recognizes the Energy Star trademark.
- Over 15,000 of the nation's buildings have been rated using the EPA's energy performance rating system.
- More than 2,000 active home builders in the United States participate in the Energy Star program.
- Energy Star's market penetration has reached more than 20% in several markets.
- One-third of the top 100 builders in the United States are Energy Star partners, and the Army Corps of Engineers now builds all new Army homes according to Energy Star guidelines.
- Almost 12,000 organizations have worked with the EPA, including over 425 public organizations, over 880 businesses across the commercial and industrial sectors, and over 8,000 small businesses.[2]

Energy Star is probably best known for its association with appliances. An appliance with an Energy Star label typically produces energy savings of 10% to 40% compared to a similar appliance that does not carry the label.

Energy Star requires that new homes be at least 15% more energy efficient than homes built to the 2004 International Residential Code (IRC) and include additional energy-saving features that typically make them 20%–30% more efficient than standard homes. The IRC is part of the International Code Council (ICC), a membership association dedicated to building safety and fire prevention. The Council develops the codes used to construct residential and commercial buildings, including homes and schools.

Energy Star home program requirements can be broken down into the following categories:

- Effective insulation
- High-performance windows
- Tight construction and ducts

---

2. EPA, *Energy Star—The Power to Protect the Environment through Energy Efficiency*. Available at www.energystar.gov. Direct link: http://www.energystar.gov/ia/partners/downloads/energy_star_report_aug_2003.pdf/.

- Efficient heating and cooling equipment
- Efficient products
- Third-party verification

Effective Insulation

While the amount of insulation is an important factor, insulation needs to be properly installed to be effective. Energy Star requires that insulation completely blanket the home without gaps, voids, or compressions, and be in full contact with the interior air barrier. Continuous sealing of the air barrier along the insulation is also critical to protect against moisture damage caused by warm air flow through the insulation to colder surfaces where it condenses.

Insulation retards the flow of heat. Heat flows through any element to cooler areas, but thermal resistance makes this process take longer. The measure of thermal resistance is called an "R-value." The higher the R-value, the better a material is at restraining heat flow.

Depending on the location of a house and its climate, walls and floors might be insulated to something in the range of R-11 to R-19 in a moderate climate. Extreme climates might call for R-values in the range of R-19 to R-25. Because heat rises, ceilings need to be well insulated. Houses in a moderate climate might have ceilings insulated between R-19 and R-30. Extreme climates might call for ceiling insulation between R-30 and R-56.

For perspective, consider that an inch of solid wood has an R-value of about 1, so insulation with an R-value of 13 is roughly the equivalent of heat having to pass through 13 inches of solid wood.

Exhibit 2.1 illustrates typical places in a house where conditioned air (and money) leaks out and unconditioned air (either hot or cold) comes in; these are areas where insulation and sealants need to be concentrated.

High-Performance Windows

Windows can make a significant difference in the energy efficiency of a house. Replacing old windows with new, energy-efficient windows is the most common type of green remodeling project. Many local utility companies offer rebates and incentives for window replacement.

Energy Star-qualified windows help keep homes cooler in the summer and warmer in the winter. They can block at least 70% of the solar heat gain in the summer and reflect radiant heat indoors during the winter. These windows also block ultraviolet sunlight, which can discolor carpets and furnishings.

Exhibit 2.1 Air Flow in a Typical Home

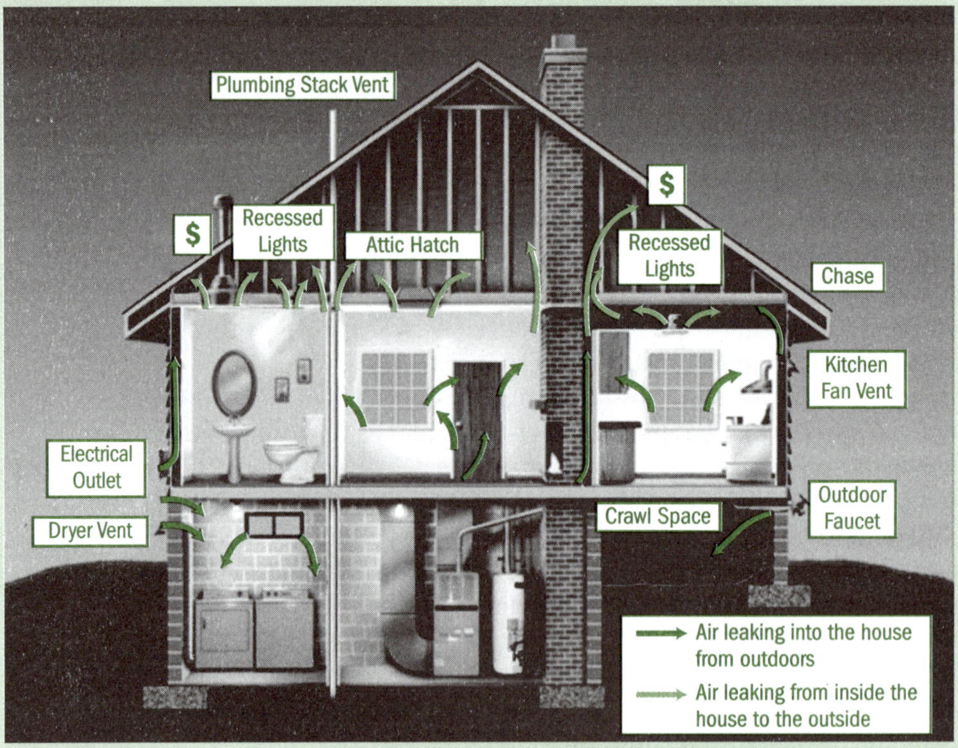

Source: Energy Star, www.energystar.gov

The advanced technologies employed by energy-efficient windows include

- Protective coatings
- Improved frames
- Invisible glass coatings
- Vacuum-sealed spaces filled with inert gas between panes
- Improved framing materials
- Improved weather stripping
- Warm edge spacers

Exhibit 2.2 depicts the composition of a modern energy-efficient window.

The first ingredient in an energy-efficient window is multiple glazings. Single-pane glass has an R-value of only R-0.5; this is actually not much better than a hole in the wall. If the surrounding wall has been insulated to R-13 or so, it would only make sense to install an energy-saving window. Double-paned windows with a space in between still only have an R-value of about R-1.5; this is three times as good as a single-pane window, but still weak. Three panes of glass that have a gas filling in between each pane produce results of up to about R-4.5. The typical filling used is argon gas, which is clear, nontoxic, and odorless. Krypton gas is also used. Krypton is more expensive but has better thermal performance.

Exhibit 2.2 Energy-Efficient Window

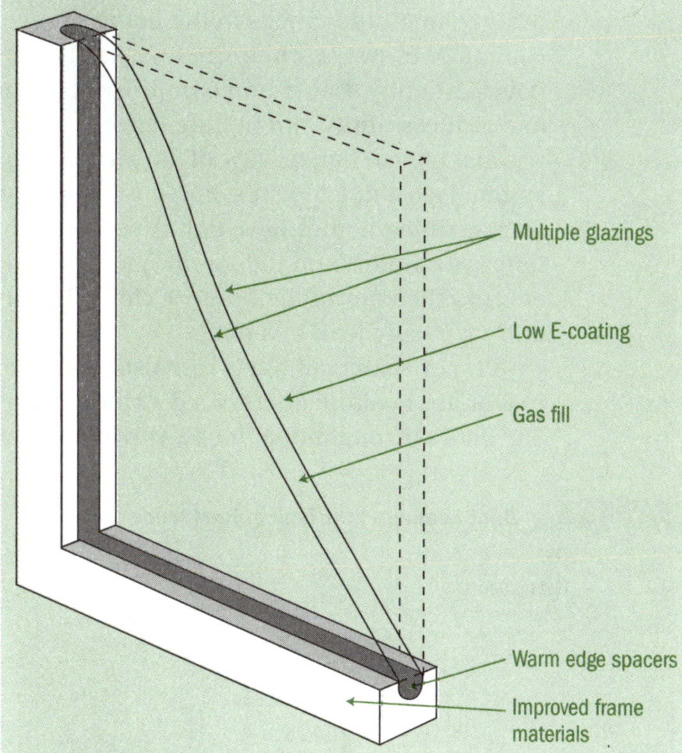

Source: Energy Star

Low-emittance (Low-E) coatings are microscopically thin metal coatings that are applied to glass to block radiant heat flow. Almost 60% of the sun's rays are infrared light. When this light passes through window glass and strikes an object (such as a piece of furniture or a wall), it warms the object and the object then gives off heat energy. This radiant energy warms the air in the room, which is good in cold weather but objectionable in hot weather.

Low-E coatings can be applied to either side or both sides of the glass to reflect certain parts of the light spectrum back out or back into a house. They were introduced in the 1980s for use in northern climes with the purpose of letting infrared rays through to increase solar gain in the winter and reflecting radiant heat back inside when it tries to escape through the glass.

Low-E windows designed for warmer climates were introduced in the 1990s. These blocked up to 40% of the solar gain and required less cooling of the interior. Improved spacers and framing materials keep the interior glass surfaces warmer, which reduces condensation on the glass and window sills. This helps to prevent possible mold growth and retards heat loss.

Tight Construction and Ducts

Sealing holes and cracks in the home's "envelope" and in heating and cooling duct systems helps reduce drafts, moisture, dust, pollen, and noise. A tightly sealed home improves comfort and indoor air quality and reduces utility and maintenance.

In a typical house, 20% of the air that moves through the duct system is lost due to leaks, holes, and poor connections. Energy Star-qualified homes have tightly sealed and well-insulated ducts to improve comfort and indoor air quality as well as increase the overall energy efficiency of the home. Exhibit 2.3 illustrates the places where ducts typically leak in a home.

Proper sealing of ducts can also help to improve the quality of indoor air. Leaking ducts can distribute dust, moisture, pollen, mold, and odors throughout a house. Obviously, leaking ducts also cause the heating and cooling systems to work harder and consume more energy.

Exhibit 2.3 **Duct Leakage in a Typical Residence**

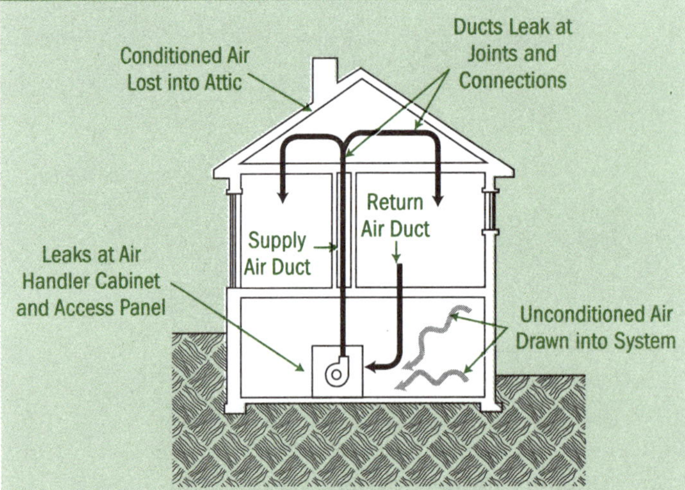

Source: Energy Star

Ducts should be run through conditioned spaces as much as possible. They are not as effective when they run through unheated or uncooled crawl spaces, basements, and attics. When ducts cannot be run through conditioned spaces, the ducts should be insulated.

Efficient Heating and Cooling Equipment

Energy-efficient heating and cooling systems can be quieter and make a home more comfortable. The Energy Star label can be found on high-efficiency furnaces, boilers, and air conditioners. Programmable thermostats are another way to conserve energy.

Heating and cooling systems need to be sized properly. Undersized systems may not be able to achieve desired temperature ranges and consume more energy struggling to do so. Oversized systems are not the answer either; they cost more initially to install and then run in shorter cycles, which does not allow the unit to reach efficient operation. Professional assistance is needed to solve this problem.

Mechanical ventilation should also be provided to bring in fresh air. Otherwise, indoor air can become stale, and moisture, odors, allergens, carbon dioxide, and other pollutants can build up. Mechanical ventilation systems include fans, ducts, and air exchangers. Proper ventilation goes hand in hand with proper insulation.

Without mechanical ventilation, air leaking into the house may come from undesirable areas, such as the garage. Mechanical ventilation systems allow for a constant flow of outside air into the home and can also provide filtration and dehumidification or humidification of the incoming outside air.

Mechanical exhaust systems can include local exhaust fans in the kitchen and bath areas, as well as attic or whole house fans. Heat and energy recovery ventilators will be discussed in Chapter 3.

Efficient Products

Energy Star homes are usually equipped with Energy Star-qualified products, including lighting fixtures, compact fluorescent bulbs, ventilation fans, and appliances such as refrigerators, dishwashers, and washing machines. The following are some statistics on Energy Star appliances:

- Energy Star-qualified refrigerators use up to 40% less energy than conventional models sold in 2001 and at least 15% less energy than models built to current federal standards. These refrigerators feature high-efficiency compressors, improved insulation, and more precise temperature and defrost mechanisms.
- Energy Star-qualified dishwashers use at least 41% less energy than the federal minimum standard for energy consumption. These dishwashers use "smart" features such as effective washing action, energy-efficient motors, and sensors that determine the necessary cycle length and water temperature.
- Energy Star-qualified clothes washers use 40%-50% less energy and about 55% less water than standard washers. These appliances have the potential to save their owners up to $50 per year on utility and water bills, in addition to savings from using less detergent. Most Energy Star washers extract more water during the spin cycle, providing further energy savings from shorter drying times in the clothes dryer.

Exhibit 2.4 compares the lifetime operating costs of an Energy Star clothes washer with a standard clothes washer. Energy Star-qualified lighting fixtures can also save money, as shown in Exhibit 2.5.

Exhibit 2.4 **Residential Clothes Washer Lifetime Operating Costs**

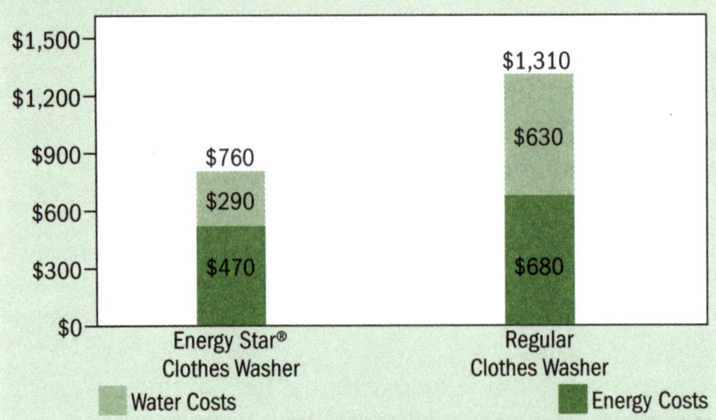

Though it may seem cheaper at first, a regular clothes washer can cost $550 more to operate over its life compared to an Energy Star clothes washer.

Source: Energy Star

Exhibit 2.5 **Lighting Fixture Operating Costs**

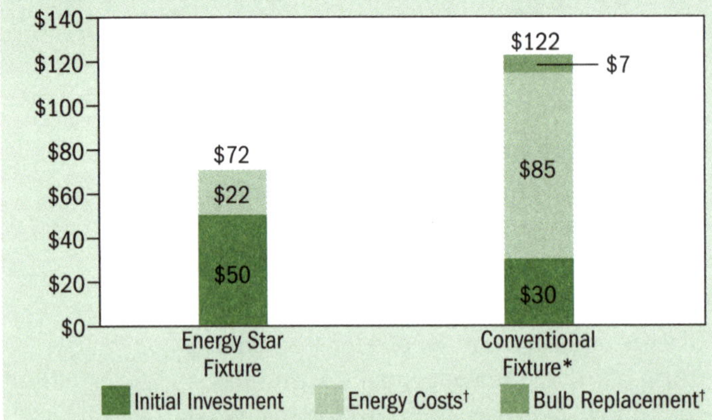

* Conventional fixture = 100 watts, Energy Star fixture = 26 watts

† Comparisons are based on a qualified fixture's pin-based bulb's lifetime of 10,000 hours (about 7 years with an average use of 3.5 hours per day) and an incandescent bulb's lifetime of 1,000 hours at $0.85 per kilowatt-hour.

Based on information from Energy Star.

Tankless water heaters are very efficient. They only run and heat water on demand, while conventional water heaters keep water heated to the proper temperature 24 hours a day. Water heaters will be discussed in more detail in Chapter 4.

Heat pump water heaters are extremely efficient. They operate with a small heat pump mounted on the top of the water tank and can save over $300 per year for a family of three compared to a conventional electric water heater. The payback period is about three years.

A solar water heater can produce the greatest amount of savings, depending on where the home is located. It may also qualify for government or utility company rebates. Exhibit 2.6 compares high-efficiency water heaters.

Third-Party Verification

Third-party verification of a home's energy efficiency is mandatory for earning the Energy Star label. The third-party verification program is a quality assurance program that checks the work of participating contractors to verify that program standards are met. Energy Star builders

Exhibit 2.6 High-Efficiency Water Heaters Compared

Water Heater Type	Energy Savings vs. Minimum Standards	Best Climates	Expected Energy Savings Over Equipment Lifetime	Expected Lifetime	Major Advantages
High-efficiency storage (tank) (oil, gas, electric)	10%-20%	Any	Up to $500	8-10 years	Lowest initial cost
Demand (tankless) using gas or electricity	45%-60%	Any	Up to $1,800	20 years	Unlimited supply of hot water
Heat pump	65% (compared to electric resistance)	Mild to hot	Up to $900	10 years	Most efficient electric fuel option
Solar with electric back-up	70%-90%	Mild to hot	Up to $2,200	20 years	Largest energy savings using a renewable energy source

Based on information from Energy Star.

employ independent "home energy raters" to choose the most appropriate energy-saving features for their homes. These raters also conduct on-site testing and inspections to verify the energy-efficiency measures taken as well as insulation, air tightness, and duct-sealing details.

Third-party verification is an important part of the Energy Star program because it allows for a neutral third party with expertise in building systems to make an independent inspection and evaluation of a property. It provides a higher level of integrity and should provide consumer protection.

To become a Certified Home Energy Rater, one must take a four-day course approved by the Residential Energy Services Network (RESNET) and provided by a RESNET-accredited provider. The candidate must then perform two ratings, including software operations, in the presence of trainers. Certified raters must also pass examinations that demonstrate a practical, working ability to effectively use the knowledge and skill set contained in the national home energy rating standard. In addition, they must pass a national test. Certified raters subscribe to a code of ethics and complete continuing education requirements.

The two possible paths to qualifying a home to meet Energy Star guidelines for energy efficiency are

1. The "performance path," a home energy rating in which software is used to model the home's energy use to verify that it meets a target score
2. The "prescriptive path," a builder option package in which builders construct the home using a prescribed set of construction specifications that meet program requirements

Both paths require independent verification and completion of a "thermal bypass inspection checklist" by a qualified home energy rater. To complete this checklist, the rater performs a comprehensive visual inspection of building details where thermal bypass (the movement of heat around or through insulation) frequently occurs due to missing air barriers or gaps between the air barrier and insulation.

Exhibit 2.7 shows a portion of the Energy Star thermal bypass inspection checklist. The entire checklist can be found in Appendix C at the end of this book.

Some steps that must be completed by an independent home energy rater when inspecting a home include

- Determining the climate zone of the home according to where it is located
- Determining envelope leakage

Exhibit 2.7

ENERGY STAR Qualified Homes
Thermal Bypass Inspection Checklist

Home Address:______________________ City:______________ State:______

Thermal Bypass	Inspection Guidelines	Corrections Needed	Builder Verified	Rater Verified	N/A
1. Overall Air Barrier and Thermal Barrier Alignment	**Requirements:** Insulation shall be installed in full contact with sealed interior and exterior air barrier except for alternate to interior air barrier under item no. 2 *(Walls Adjoining Exterior Walls or Unconditioned Spaces)*				
	All Climate Zones:				
	1.1 Overall Alignment Throughout Home	☐	☐	☐	☐
	1.2 Garage Band Joist Air Barrier (at bays adjoining conditioned space)	☐	☐	☐	☐
	1.3 Attic Eave Baffles Where Vents/Leakage Exist	☐	☐	☐	☐
	Only at Climate Zones 4 and Higher:				
	1.4 Slab-edge Insulation (A maximum of 25% of the slab edge may be uninsulated in Climate Zones 4 and 5.)	☐	☐	☐	☐
	Best Practices Encouraged, Not Req'd.:				
	1.5 Air Barrier At All Band Joists (Climate Zones 4 and higher)	☐	☐	☐	☐
	1.6 Minimize Thermal Bridging (e.g., OVE framing, SIPs, ICFs)	☐	☐	☐	☐
2. Walls Adjoining Exterior Walls or Unconditioned Spaces	**Requirements:** • Fully insulated wall aligned with air barrier at both interior and exterior, **OR** • Alternate for **Climate Zones 1 thru 3**, sealed exterior air barrier aligned with RESNET Grade 1 insulation fully supported • Continuous top and bottom plates or sealed blocking				
	2.1 Wall Behind Shower/Tub	☐	☐	☐	☐
	2.2 Wall Behind Fireplace	☐	☐	☐	☐
	2.3 Insulated Attic Slopes/Walls	☐	☐	☐	☐
	2.4 Attic Knee Walls	☐	☐	☐	☐
	2.5 Skylight Shaft Walls	☐	☐	☐	☐
	2.6 Wall Adjoining Porch Roof	☐	☐	☐	☐
	2.7 Staircase Walls	☐	☐	☐	☐
	2.8 Double Walls	☐	☐	☐	☐
3. Floors between Conditioned and Exterior Spaces	**Requirements:** • Air barrier is installed at any exposed fibrous insulation edges • Insulation is installed to maintain permanent contact with sub-floor above including necessary supports (e.g., staves for blankets, netting for blown-in) • Blanket insulation is verified to have no gaps, voids or compression. • Blown-in insulation is verified to have proper density with firm packing				
	3.1 Insulated Floor Above Garage	☐	☐	☐	☐
	3.2 Cantilevered Floor	☐	☐	☐	☐

Source: Energy Star

- Sealing and testing ducts
- Verifying that Energy Star-qualified windows, appliances, and ventilation fans are being used in the home
- Verifying that heating and cooling systems in the home are sized according to Energy Star specifications
- Completing the thermal bypass inspection checklist

To qualify for Energy Star's official blue label, a home must score at least 75 points on a scale of 100. This blue label is usually found on a home's electrical breaker box and is shown in Exhibit 2.8.

Energy Star homes are not universal but are quite popular in some parts of the United States such as Texas, the East Coast, metropolitan areas of the Midwest, Colorado, California, and the Pacific Northwest. The map in Exhibit 2.9 shows the locations of Energy Star-qualified homes as of 2007. The graph in Exhibit 2.10 shows the overall growth of Energy Star's popularity in the Southwest. This graph shows that there is a substantial market share for Energy Star homes in some areas. In 2005, for example, more than 40% of new homes in Nevada and more than 30% of new homes in Texas were classified as energy efficient by Energy Star.

Exhibit 2.8 Energy Star Label

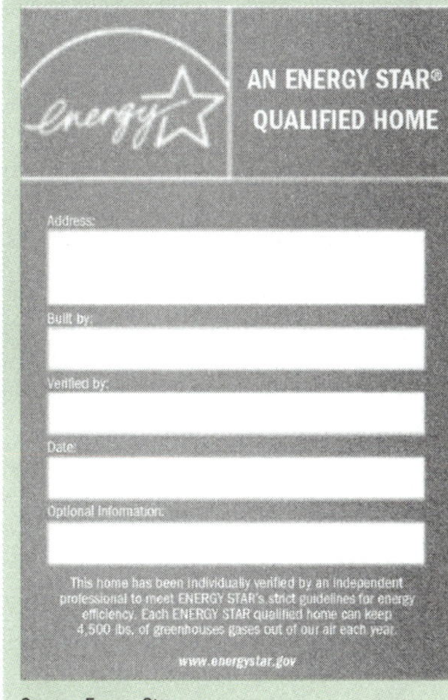

Source: Energy Star

A third-party home energy rater performs a blower door test to measure the amount of insulation provided by the exterior door. Photo appears courtesy of Energy Star.

NAHB National Green Building Standard

The National Association of Home Builders (NAHB) has had a set of guidelines for green home building in place since 2004. The original guidelines were known as the NAHB Model Green Home Building Guidelines. In 2007, the NAHB and the International Code Council (ICC) announced their agreement to develop and publish the NAHB National Green Building Standard in order to establish a much needed and nationally recognizable standard

Exhibit 2.9 **Locations of Energy Star Homes**

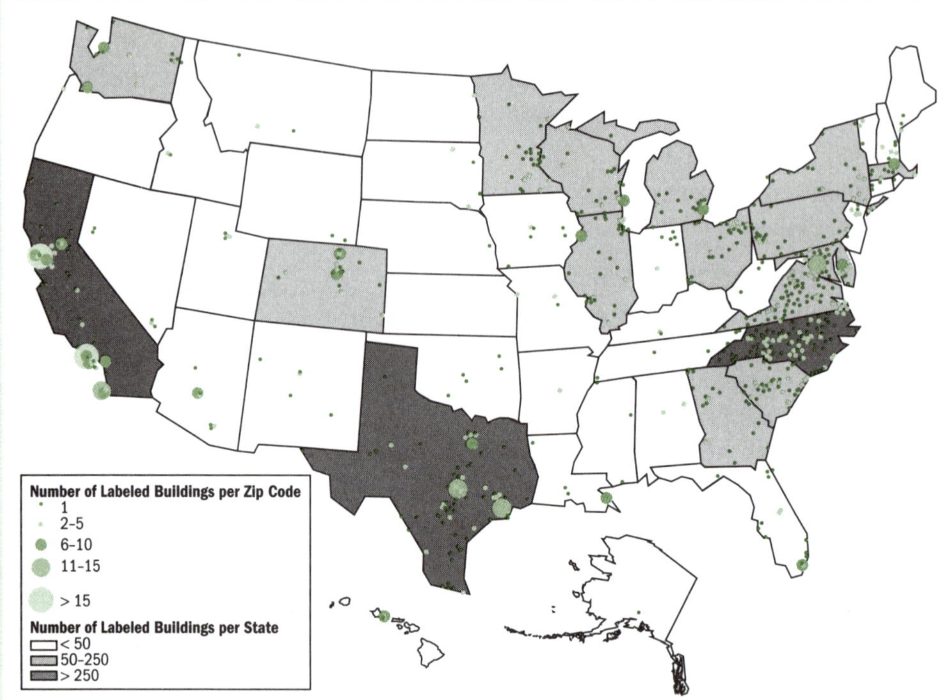

Source: Energy Star

Exhibit 2.10 **Energy Star Market Share for New Homes in the Southwest**

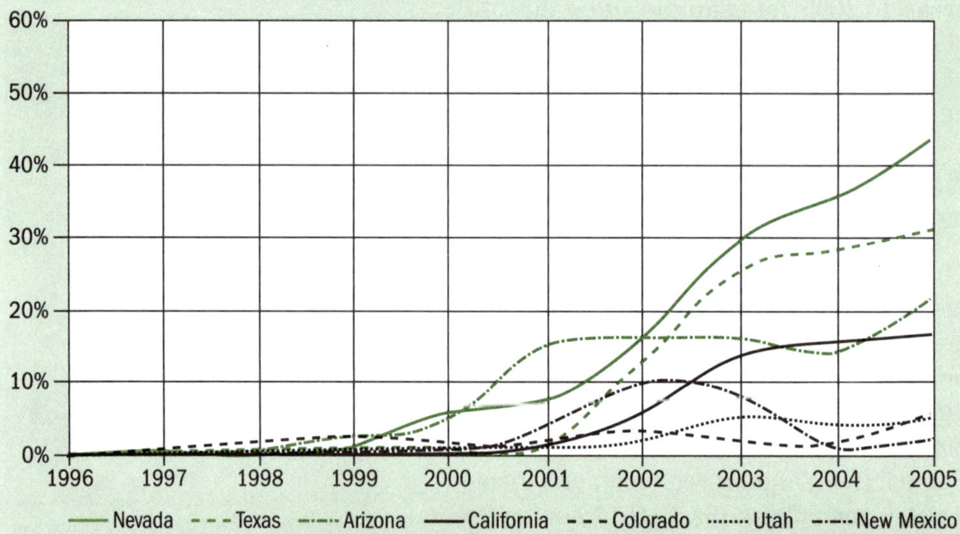

Source: Energy Star

definition of "green building." The new standard builds on the 2004 guidelines and covers single-unit and multi-unit homes, residential remodeling projects, and site development projects.[3]

According to the National Green Building Standard, a builder, remodeler, or developer must incorporate a minimum number of features in the following areas:

- Site design and development
- Lot design, preparation, and development
- Resource, energy, and water efficiency
- Indoor environmental quality
- Operation, maintenance, and building owner education

The more points accrued in each area, the higher the score. The score determines if the building can qualify for a "bronze," "silver," "gold," or "emerald" rating. Exhibit 2.11 outlines the number of points needed in each category to qualify for each rating level.

An interesting part of the NAHB National Green Building Standard is that its green building practices are customized for different parts of the country. Included in the standard is a map depicting the different climate zones of the United States. Requirements can be

Exhibit 2.11 NAHB National Green Building Standard Requirements

Threshold Point Ratings for Green Buildings

Green Building Categories	Performance Point Levels *† BRONZE	SILVER	GOLD	EMERALD
1. Lot design, preparation, and development	39	66	93	119
2. Resource efficiency	45	79	113	146
3. Energy efficiency	30	60	100	120
4. Water efficiency	14	26	41	60
5. Indoor environmental quality	36	65	100	140
6. Operation, maintenance, and building owner education	8	10	11	12
7. Additional points from any category	50	100	100	100
Total points	222	406	558	697

* In addition to the threshold number of points in each category, all mandatory provisions of each category shall be implemented.

† For dwelling units greater than 4,000 square feet (372 square meters), the number of points in Category 7 (additional points from any category) shall be increased in accordance with Section 601.1. The "total points" shall be increased by the same number of points.

Threshold Point Ratings for Site Design and Development

Green Subdivision Category	Performance Point Levels One Star	Two Stars	Three Stars	Four Stars
Site design and development	79	104	134	175

Based on infromation from the NAHB National Green Building Program, www.nahbgreen.org.

3. Much of the information in this section has been gathered from the NAHB National Green Building Program Web site, www.nahbgreen.org.

modified according to the heating and cooling loads expected within each zone. Varying amounts of points are then awarded in categories such as building thermal envelope, windows, and furnace/boiler efficiency.

While the Energy Star program concentrates solely on the energy efficiency of the building, the NAHB National Green Building Standard is more comprehensive. In addition to energy efficiency, the NAHB National Green Building Standard also mandates green building practices that relate to the site, resource efficiency, water efficiency, and indoor environmental quality. The Leadership in Energy and Environmental Design (LEED) program of the USGBC, which will be discussed in the next chapter, also has a similar scope.

Residential Energy Services Network

Some of the measurements referred to in the NAHB National Green Building Standard are based on standards of the Residential Energy Services Network (RESNET). RESNET, a nonprofit membership corporation, serves as a national standards making body for energy-efficiency rating systems. RESNET is used by the mortgage industry for capitalizing energy efficiency in mortgages. It is also used by the federal government for the verification of building energy performance in

- Federal tax credit qualification
- Energy Star homes
- The U.S. Department of Energy's Building America program
- Minimum code compliance for 16 states

According to RESNET, www.natresnet.org, the organization uses a relative energy-use index known as the Home Energy Rating System (HERS). A HERS index of 100 represents the energy use of an "American standard new home," while an index of zero indicates that the proposed building uses no net purchased energy (a "zero-energy building"), as shown in Exhibit 2.12.

RESNET's "American standard new home" is one that would meet the International Code Council's minimum standards. The HERS Index is calculated using accredited building simulation software tools. Buildings are rated by certified raters and rec-

Exhibit 2.12 HERS Index

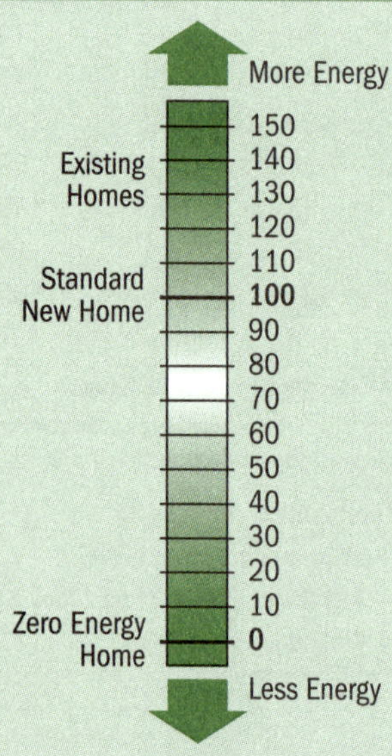

Source: RESNET, www.natresnet.org

ommendations are presented for cost-effective improvements. HERS indices may be useful when comparing various green buildings. They are a standard measure of energy efficiency. When appraising a green home, it is useful to ask for its HERS rating, if one has been done. Any Energy Star home, NAHB National Green Building Standard-rated home, or LEED-certified home must have achieved a HERS rating as part of the certification process. For example, a home with a HERS index of 75 is 10% more energy efficient than one with an index of 85; this could be used as the basis for an adjustment in the sales comparison approach.

Local Green Building Programs

Local green building initiatives have been around for more than 15 years. Some of these programs are affiliated with home building organizations, while others are affiliated with public sector and nonprofit organizations. Local green building programs are voluntary in nature and market-driven. Both the EPA and NAHB provide information about local green building programs on their Web sites, www.epa.gov and www.nahbgreen.org.[4]

Local programs obviously emphasize different aspects of energy efficiency depending on their geographical location. For example, cooling efficiency is considered to be more important in Florida, while more emphasis is placed on insulation and heating efficiency in Minnesota. Other local factors might include the availability of recycled materials and tax credits or rebate programs offered by local government or utility companies.

Seattle Area Built Green Program

The Seattle Area Built Green program is a good example of a local green building initiave. Built Green is a nonprofit, residential building program of the Master Builders Association (MBA) of King and Snohomish counties and was developed in partnership with the counties and other agencies in Washington State. This program is based on a checklist approach.[5]

To be able to use the trademarked title of a "Built Green" home through this program, a builder must first register the home and then accumulate points based on the provided checklist. Specialized checklists are available for single-unit new homes, additions and renovations of existing projects, apartments and condominiums,

4. From the NAHB's home page at www.nahbgreen.org, click on "Find a Local Program" under "Quick Links."
5. Information for this section has been gathered from the Seattle Area Built Green Web site, www.builtgreen.net.

and neighborhoods and developments. These checklists include six categories of environmentally friendly items.

1. Green building codes
2. Site and water protection
3. Energy efficiency
4. Health and air quality
5. Materials efficiency
6. Environmentally responsible home ownership

After construction is completed, the builder sends a signed copy of the checklist to the MBA, certifying that the home contains the items identified in the checklist. Based on the builder certification, the MBA awards the appropriate certificate of merit for a one-, two-, three-, four-, or five-star rating. The first three categories are based solely on the builder's certification from the signed checklist. The four- and five-star ratings require inspection by a third-party verifier who subscribes to a code of ethics.

Since 2000, the Seattle Area Built Green program has certified over 14,600 homes. It certified more than 1,000 homes in 2009 alone. Seattle Area Built Green also sponsors education programs and courses. The Built Green program can also be found in other areas of the country, such as Colorado.

International Green Building Programs

The United Kingdom's Building Research Establishment's Environmental Assessment Method (BREEAM) is recognized as the world's most established environmental assessment method for buildings.

Since 2008, it has been mandatory that all new homes constructed in England have a rating from the Code for Sustainable Homes. The code is an environmental assessment method for new homes based on the Building Research Establishment's requirements and contains mandatory performance levels in seven key areas. Assessments for the code are made initially during the design phase based on drawings, plans, and specifications, and assessments and certifications are then made again after construction is completed.

CHAPTER 3

LEED for Homes

Introduction

The Leadership in Energy and Environmental Design (LEED) Green Building Rating System is a third-party certification program and the nationally accepted benchmark for the design, construction, and operation of high-performance green buildings. LEED was developed by the U.S. Green Building Council (USGBC) to provide building owners and operators with a concise framework for identifying and implementing practical and measurable green building design, construction, operations, and maintenance solutions. The USGBC has become one of the leading organizations in the green building movement due to the success of the LEED rating system. Over 18,000 organizations from the building industry belong to the USGBC; members include building owners and users, developers, facility managers, architects, designers, engineers, general contractors, subcontractors, product and building system manufacturers, government agencies, and nonprofit organizations.[1]

LEED is best known for its rating systems for commercial and industrial buildings. With input from a wide range of professionals, the USGBC has also created rating systems for

- New construction
- The operation and maintenance of existing buildings
- Commercial interiors
- Core and shells
- Schools
- Retail facilities

1. Much of the information in this chapter has been gathered from the USGBC Web site, www.usgbc.org.

- Health care facilities
- Neighborhood development

The newest LEED program is LEED for Homes. The official LEED for Homes Rating System was formally released in 2008. The system awards designations of "certified," "silver," "gold," and "platinum," depending on a scale of points achieved for sustainable qualities in a building's design and construction. The LEED for Homes program will be the focus of this chapter.

LEED for Homes Criteria

The LEED for Homes Rating System is a set of industry best practices intended to help builders construct better homes. LEED is holistic and its scope involves looking at the entire building as a system. The rating system identifies specific measures that may be incorporated into the building of a home. Quality builders may already include many of these measures in their work; LEED gives them industry recognition and third-party verification. The 2008 version of the LEED for Homes Rating System–the most recent version as of this book's publication–measures the overall performance of a home in eight different categories. These eight categories and their areas of focus are listed as follows:

1. **Innovation and design process**
   The use of an integrated project team, unique regional credits, and exemplary performance levels
2. **Location and linkages**
   The placement of homes in socially and environmentally responsible ways in relation to the larger community
3. **Sustainable sites**
   The use of the entire property to minimize the project's impact on the site
4. **Water efficiency**
   Indoor and outdoor water-efficient practices
5. **Energy and atmosphere**
   Energy efficiency, particularly in the building envelope and in the heating and cooling system
6. **Materials and resources**
   Selection of environmentally preferable materials and minimization of waste during construction
7. **Indoor environmental quality**
   Improvement of indoor air quality by reducing the creation of and exposure to pollutants

8. **Awareness and education**
   The education of homeowners, tenants, or building managers about the operation and maintenance of a LEED home

A high-performance home typically incorporates design strategies that result in the efficient use of resources, the selection of environmentally responsible yet high-performance materials and systems, and building practices that ensure proper installation.

Exhibit 3.1 How Does LEED Define a Green Home?

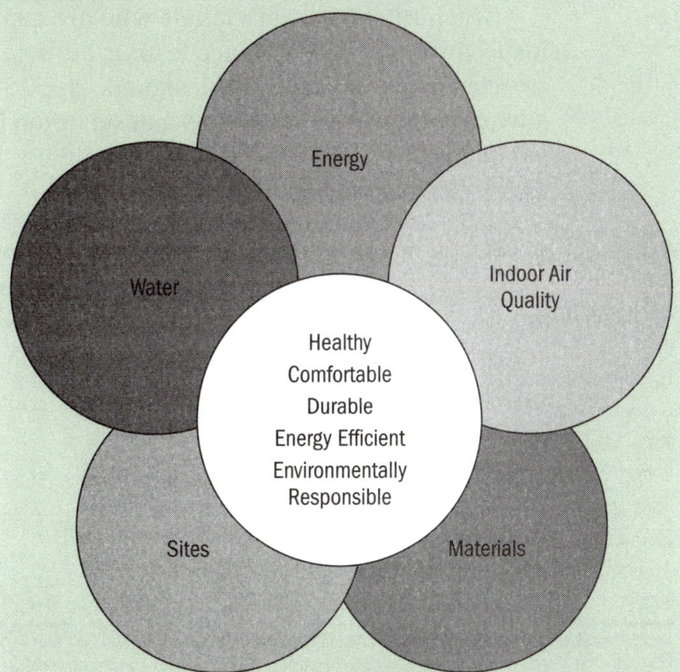

Source: USGBC, "Green Homes" PowerPoint presentation. Available at www.usgbc.org and accessed April 2010. Direct link: http://www.usgbc.org/DisplayPage.aspx?CMSPageID=1720/.

LEED for Homes Certification

Exhibit 3.2 presents a summary of the point levels required for various levels of certification under the LEED for Homes program, which vary based on the square footage of the home. Smaller, more efficient homes are rewarded in this system.

The LEED rating system contains several credits labeled as "prerequisites," which are mandatory measures that must be accomplished for any home. A total of 18 prerequisites are found in the eight major categories.

Points can be achieved through a wide variety of optional credits, giving project teams great flexibility. To achieve a certification level, all

Exhibit 3.2 LEED for Homes Certification Levels for a Four-Bedroom House

	LEED Platinum	LEED Gold	LEED Silver	LEED Certified
1,800 sq. ft.	80 pts.	65 pts.	50 pts.	35 pts.
2,600 sq. ft.	90 pts.	75 pts.	60 pts.	45 pts.
5,200 sq. ft.	108 pts.	93 pts.	78 pts.	63 pts.

Source: USGBC, "About LEED" PowerPoint presentation. Available at www.usgbc.org and accessed April 2010. Direct link:: http://www.usgbc.org/Display Page.aspx?CMS Page ID=1720/.

of the prerequisites must be met, plus a certain amount of optional credits must be earned. A total of 67 optional credits are available; however, a minimum number of points must be earned in certain credit categories. Exhibit 3.3 summarizes the point requirements in each category.

The strength of the LEED program is third-party verification by LEED for Homes providers and green raters. LEED for Homes providers consist of local and regional organizations that are chosen by the USGBC to provide quality control and certification services to LEED for Homes projects.

Green raters are individuals who are qualified to perform field inspections and performance testing, ensuring that homes are constructed as well as they are designed. The USGBC has developed advanced education as well as a designation for green home designers and consultants who can assist builders. These professionals hold the "LEED AP + Homes" designation.

Exhibit 3.3 **LEED for Homes Prerequisites and Minimum Point Requirements**

Credit Category	Prerequisite Measures (Mandatory)	Minimum Point Requirements	Maximum Points Available
Innovation & design process	3	0	11
Location & linkages	0	0	10
Sustainable sites	2	5	22
Water efficiency	0	3	15
Energy & atmosphere	2	0	38
Materials & resources	3	2	16
Indoor environmental quality	7	6	21
Awareness & education	1	0	3
Total	18	16	136

Based on information from the USGBC's *LEED for Homes Rating System*, January 2008 ed. (USGBC, 2007). This document is available at www.usgbc.org. Direct link: http://www.usgbc.org/ShowFile.aspx?DocumentID=03638/. Information accessed April 2010. Note that updates to the rating system are made on an ongoing basis.

LEED for Homes Rating System

The USGBC provides a checklist for the LEED for Homes Rating System to be filled out by the responsible party, such as the builder, engineer, or architect who completed the building design.[2] This form attests to the completion of individual measures and compliance with the requirements for certification. A sample of part of this checklist appears in Exhibit 3.4. The entire checklist can be found in Appendix D at the end of this book.

2. Much of the information in this section has been gathered from the January 2008 edition of the USGBC's *LEED for Homes Rating System* (USGBC, 2007). This document is available at www.usgbc.org. Direct link: http://www.usgbc.org/ShowFile.aspx?DocumentID=3638/. Information accessed April 2010. Note that updates to the rating system are made on an ongoing basis.

Exhibit 3.4

LEED for Homes Checklist

Builder Name:	
Project Team Leader (if different):	
Home Address (Street/City/State):	

Project Description:

				Adjusted Certification Thresholds			
Building Type:		Project type:		Certified:	*45.0*	Gold:	*75.0*
# of Bedrooms:	*0*	Floor Area:	*0.0*	Silver:	*60.0*	Platinum:	*90.0*

Project Point Total: 0	ID: 0	SS: 0	EA: 0	EQ: 0	
Certification Level: Not Certified	LL: 0	WE: 0	MR: 0	AE: 0	

Notes:
1. Detailed information on measures below are provided in the LEED for Homes Rating System
2. ✎ Indicates measures that must be documented using the Accountability Form

				Max Points Available	Project Points Y / Pts	No	Maybe
Innovation and Design Process (ID) (No Minimum Points Required)							
1. Integrated Project Planning		1.1	Preliminary Rating	Prerequisite			
		1.2	Integrated Project Team	1			
		1.3	Professional Credentialed with Respect to LEED for Homes	1			
		1.4	Design Charrette	1			
		1.5	Building Orientation for Solar Design	1			
2. Durability Management Process		2.1	Durability Planning	Prerequisite			
		2.2	Durability Management	Prerequisite			
		2.3	Third-Party Durability Management Verification	3			
3. Innovative or Regional Design	✎	3.1	Innovation #1 ______	1			
	✎	3.2	Innovation #2 ______	1			
	✎	3.3	Innovation #3 ______	1			
	✎	3.4	Innovation #4 ______	1			
			Sub-Total for ID Category:	*11*	*0*		
Location and Linkages (LL) (No Minimum Points Required)			*OR*				
1. LEED ND		1	LEED for Neighborhood Development **LL2-6**	10			
2. Site Selection	✎	2	Site Selection	2			
3. Preferred Locations		3.1	Edge Development	1			
		3.2	Infill **LL 3.1**	2			
		3.3	Previously Developed	1			
4. Infrastructure		4	Existing Infrastructure	1			

Source: USGBC, *LEED for Homes Rating System*. Accessed April 2010. Note that updates to the rating system are made on an ongoing basis.

Innovation and Design Process

The first category in the LEED for Homes Rating System focuses on innovation and design. This category specifically promotes an integrated cost-effective design and construction process. Participants should take a holistic approach to this process and involve all the members of the project team, which may include

- Architects
- Mechanical and energy engineers
- Performance testers
- Civil engineers
- Builders
- Green raters
- Interior designers

An important consideration for green building is that all the relevant parties meet in advance to ensure smooth facilitation and coordination throughout the project. An integrated design team helps ensure a properly constructed and high-performing home. It is hoped that appraisers will be invited to join the project team in the near future so that they may have the opportunity to add their expertise to the planning process.

Credit points are available in this category for having a principal member of the team who is a LEED Accredited Professional with Homes specialty (LEED AP + Homes). An individual with a LEED AP + Homes designation has project experience and has passed a rigorous exam, demonstrating a thorough understanding of green building practices and principles as they relate to the LEED for Homes rating system. The professionals can be excellent information resources.

Additional credit can also be obtained for orienting the building for solar design, which means meeting very practical requirements. For example, the glazing areas on the north- and south-facing walls must be at least 50% greater than the total of the glazing on the east- and west-facing walls, and at least 90% of the glazing on the south-facing wall must be completely shaded at noon on June 21 and unshaded at noon on December 21 (shading can come from trees, overhangs, etc.). Emphasizing glazing on the north walls allows for daylighting without direct sunshine streaming into the building. For south-facing walls, designing the building so that the window areas are shaded during warm weather prevents extra heat from entering the building and reduces the cooling system's loads while allowing sunlight to enter those windows during cold weather and reduce the heating system's loads.

Next, a "durability management process" must be instituted. This type of process is intended to promote durability and high performance through appropriate materials selection and an effective design and construction process. An example of durability management is indoor moisture control in such areas as kitchens, baths, and laundry areas. If a home is located in a floodplain, what strategies are being implemented to prevent water infiltration? In a northern climate, how is heat loss being addressed? These are all durability concerns that may need to be considered. Interior designers can be very helpful in this process.

Finally, any type of innovation in green design or construction practices that has not been covered anywhere else in the rating system and that goes above the stated requirements is encouraged. These innovations would have to have a tangible and measurable effect in reducing the environmental impact of the home. They also need to be submitted for approval by review teams.

Location and Linkages

Thirteen points can be obtained by building a home in a LEED-certified Neighborhood Development (LEED ND), which is also a USGBC certification program. Projects not located in a LEED ND area can achieve points for individual credits. Some of the requirements in this program include

- Proximity to water and wastewater infrastructure
- Wetland and water body conservation
- Agricultural land conservation
- Floodplain avoidance
- Brownfield redevelopment
- Reduced automobile independence
- Proximity to housing and jobs
- Restoration of habitat

Points can also be awarded for

- Site selection
- Building in or near existing communities
- Building on previously developed land
- Building near existing infrastructure
- Building in patterns that allow for walking, biking, and public transit
- Providing open spaces

The rating system specifies that development should not occur on land with an elevation at or below the 100-year floodplain, land that is home for any endangered species, land that is within 100 feet of water (including wetlands), land that was public parkland prior to acquisition, or land that contains "prime" or "unique" soils (as identified by state Natural Resources Conservation Service soil surveys).

Building in or near existing communities and infrastructure may allow for the use of existing infrastructure, instead of requiring new construction or the extension of existing facilities. Building on previously developed land is encouraged because it is a type of recycling and does not use up undeveloped land. Building in patterns that allow for walking, biking, and public transit minimizes dependency on individual automobiles and their impact on the environment in terms of air pollution and fossil fuel use. Finally, open spaces are encouraged, as they are good for the whole community and help promote walking and outdoor physical activity. Open spaces also help cleanse the atmosphere.

Sustainable Sites

The sustainable sites category is broken down into six main subcategories:

1. Site stewardship
2. Landscaping
3. Local heat island effect
4. Surface water management
5. Nontoxic pest control
6. Compact development

Site Stewardship

The site stewardship subcategory is centered around minimizing environmental damage to the building lot during construction. Planning and implementing appropriate erosion control measures during construction is a prerequisite. One obvious strategy is to stockpile and cover topsoil from the site to be reused later. Another part of this prerequisite is to control the path and velocity of runoff with measures such as silt fences and straw bales; this can temporarily protect against erosion. Keep in mind that LEED for Homes is a national program. Erosion control measures may be standard building practices in many areas but may rarely be done in others.

Credit can be obtained in this subcategory for minimizing the disturbed area of the site. Strategies for this include developing a tree and plant preservation plan or leaving at least 40% of the buildable lot area undisturbed.

Landscaping

The focus of the landscaping subcategory is on designing landscape features to avoid invasive species and to minimize the demand for water and synthetic chemicals. Introducing no invasive plant species is a prerequisite. An *invasive species* is an alien species whose introduction does or is likely to cause economic or environmental harm or harm to human health. An example of an invasive species is the kudzu vine, which is found in the Southeastern region of the United States.

Credit in this subcategory can be obtained for basic landscape design, which includes common practices such as using drought-tolerant turf or not using turf in shaded areas or areas with a slope of more than 25% to cut down on water use. Credit is also given for limiting the use of conventional grass, installing drought-tolerant plants, and reducing overall irrigation by at least 20%.

Local Heat Island Effect

The third subcategory under site stewardship centers around designing landscape features that reduce local heat island effects. As discussed in Chapter 1, the heat island effect is what happens when solar energy retention on constructed surfaces (sidewalks, streets, etc.) causes warmer temperatures. This is a real fact of life in urban areas and densely settled suburban areas.

Credit in this subcategory can be earned by locating trees to provide shade for 50% of all sidewalks, patios, and driveways within 50 feet of the home or installing light-colored, high-albedo materials or vegetation for at least 50% of sidewalks, patios, and driveways within 50 feet of the home. Light-colored materials tend to reflect light and dark-colored materials absorb light and create heat. Typical blacktop or asphalt materials absorb large quantities of solar heat, even on cloudy days. *Albedo* is synonymous with *solar reflectance*, which is defined by the USGBC as "the ratio of the reflected solar energy to the incoming solar energy over wavelengths of approximately 0.3 to 2.5 micrometers. A reflectance of 100% means that all of the energy striking a reflecting surface is reflected back into the atmosphere and none of the energy is absorbed by the surface."[3]

Recommended materials to counter local heat island effects include

- White or gray concrete
- Open pavers with spaces for ground cover
- Reflective roofing materials
- Any materials with a solar reflective index of at least 29%

The solar reflective index (SRI) is defined by the USGBC as "a measure of a material's ability to reject solar heat, as shown by a small temperature rise. It is defined so that standard black has an SRI of 0% and standard white has an SRI of 100%. For example, a standard black surface has a temperature rise of 90° F in full sun and a standard white surface has a temperature rise of 14.6° F."[4]

Practically speaking, the higher a material's SRI, the cooler that material remains. For example, traditional roofing materials have an SRI of between 5% (brown shingles) and 20% (green shingles). White shingles with an SRI of about 35% were popular in the 1960s, but they lost favor because they got dirty easily. The current trend is to make white shingles more reflective and self-cleaning so they stay

3. USGBC, *New Construction & Major Renovation Reference Guide*, Version 2.2, 3rd ed. (October 2007).
4. Ibid.

Exhibit 3.5 **Potential Savings from Improving Roof Reflectivity**

City	Potential Savings
Phoenix	$37 million
Los Angeles	$35 million
Houston	$27 million
Dallas/Fort Worth	$20 million
Miami/Ft. Lauderdale	$20 million
New York City	$16 million
Chicago	$10 million
Atlanta	$9 million
New Orleans	$9 million
Washington, D.C./Baltimore	$8 million
Philadelphia	$3 million

Based on information from the E. O. Lawrence Berkeley National Laboratory, Environmental Energy Technologies Division, Heat Island Group, http://eetd.lbl.gov/HeatIsland/CoolRoofs/.

whiter. Some roofing materials with a high SRI are also known as "cool roofs" and have the Energy Star product certification.

While an individual building may not counter the heat island effect by itself, the potential energy savings en masse could be powerful. Exhibit 3.5 shows the potential net energy savings from improving roof reflectivity across the nation. The net savings in this case are the savings of cooling energy use less the penalties of heating energy use.

For homes in cold climates, studies have shown that the summer energy savings from a reflective roof outweigh any heating penalties that result from having a light-colored roof in the winter as opposed to a more traditional dark roof.[5]

Surface Water Management

Managing stormwater runoff is a big concern, especially in urban areas and older areas where rainwater and household sewage is combined. A heavy downpour can fill these combined systems to capacity, creating public health dangers. The surface water management subcategory of LEED for Homes centers around designing site features that minimize erosion and runoff from the home site.

Credit can be obtained in this subcategory for designing a lot so that at least 70% of the built environment is permeable or designed to capture water runoff and let it infiltrate on the site. Water that is absorbed in the ground can be used for vegetation and trees as well as recharging underground aquifers. Stormwater runoff that leaves the site can carry away sediment, flood adjoining areas, and clog up stormwater pipes and facilities.

Other surface water management strategies include vegetated landscapes, permeable paving, and impermeable surfaces that are designed to direct runoff to a permanent infiltration feature such as a

5. Comparisons of different roofing products in different climates can be made using the Department of Energy's "cool roof calculator" at http://www.ornl.gov/sci/roofs+walls/facts/CoolCalcEnergy.htm/.

low, vegetated tract of land called a *rain garden* or a rainwater storage tank. Permeable pavement allows water to infiltrate through its surface. Examples of permeable paving will be illustrated in Chapter 4.

Credit can also be obtained for designing and installing permanent erosion control measures such as terraces, retaining walls, or trees and groundcovers. Credit is also given for designing and installing measures to manage roof runoff, such as using dry wells or tanks or installing a vegetated roof on at least 50% of the structure.

Nontoxic Pest Control

The focus of the nontoxic pest control subcategory is on encouraging the design of home features that minimize the need for poisons to control insects, rodents, and other pests. Participants can gain credit in this subcategory for implementing pest control alternatives, such as keeping all wood at least 12 inches above the soil or sealing all external cracks, joints, penetrations, edges, and entry points with caulking.

Compact Development

The last subcategory of site stewardship is designed to encourage the use of compact development patterns to conserve land and promote community livability, transportation efficiency, and walkability. Credit can be obtained by building in areas with moderate, high-, or very high-density homes. For example, homes with an average housing density of at least seven dwelling units per acre of buildable land would qualify as "moderate density," while homes with an average housing density of 20 or more dwelling units per acre of buildable land would qualify as "very high density." This helps encourage development on urban infill lots rather than on undeveloped land tracts.

Water Efficiency

The water efficiency category within LEED for Homes is broken down into three subcategories.

1. Water reuse
2. Irrigation system
3. Indoor water use

Water Reuse

The water reuse subcategory is centered around promoting the use of municipal recycled water or offsetting the central water supply through the capture and controlled reuse of rainwater and/or graywater, as permitted by local plumbing codes.

Credit can be earned for designing and installing a rainwater harvesting and storage system that can be used for landscape irrigation or indoor water use. It must be sized to hold all the water from a one-inch rainfall. *Rain barrels* are a common rainwater harvesting system for homes. Credit can also be earned by using a municipal recycled water system.

A graywater reuse system can also be installed and used for landscape irrigation or non-potable indoor water use. The Uniform Plumbing Code defines *graywater* as untreated household wastewater that has not come into contact with toilet waste. This includes water from bathtubs, showers, bathroom wash basins, and clothes washers and laundry tubs, but does not include wastewater from kitchen sinks or dishwashers.[6] Graywater can replace fresh water in many instances, saving money and increasing the effective water supply in regions where irrigation is needed. Much of the water used in residential buildings is for toilets. By using graywater to fill and flush toilets instead of potable "white" water, the home's demand for water is reduced without sacrificing sanitary conditions.

Irrigation System

Landscape irrigation accounts for a tremendous amount of water in a typical residence, averaging about 50% of water use. LEED for Homes rewards homes built with systems that control and reduce or eliminate the need for irrigation.

Credit in this subcategory can be earned by installing a high-efficiency irrigation system, performing a third-party inspection of the irrigation system in operation to ensure the system does not water the driveway or turn on during a rainstorm, or reducing the overall irrigation demand by at least 45%.

Indoor Water Use

The focus of the indoor water use subcategory is the minimization of indoor demand for water through water-efficient fixtures and fittings. Credit can be obtained for installing high-efficiency or very high-efficiency fixtures or fittings.

High-efficiency fixtures and fittings must meet the following criteria:

- The average flow rate for lavatory faucets must be 2 gallons per minute or less.
- The average flow rate for showers must be 2 gallons per minute or less per stall.
- Toilets must have an average flow rate of 1.3 gallons per flush or less, be dual-flush (1.6 and 0.8 gallons per flush), or bear the EPA WaterSense label.

---

6. USGBC, *New Construction & Major Renovation Reference Guide.*

Very high-efficiency fixtures and fittings must meet or exceed the following criteria:

- Lavatory faucets must have an average flow rate of 1.5 gallons per minute or less or bear the EPA WaterSense label.
- The average flow rate for showers must be 1.75 gallons per minute or less per stall.
- The average flow rate for toilets must be 1.1 gallons per flush or less.

WaterSense is an EPA program designed to encourage water efficiency in the United States through the use of a special label on consumer products indicating that the fixture uses 20% less water than what is standard and required by code. Reducing water consumption inside and outside the home can lead to significant utility bill savings in various parts of the country where water scarcity has led to high water and sewage rates. Exhibit 3.6 compares the cost of water in different parts of the country.

Energy and Atmosphere

The energy and atmosphere category is the most important credit area in LEED for Homes, representing 30% of the available points that can be earned. It is divided into 11 subcategories.

1. Optimize energy performance
2. Insulation
3. Air infiltration
4. Windows
5. Duct tightness

Exhibit 3.6 2008 Cost of Water per 1,000 Gallons in the United States

City	Water	Sewer	Total
Fairbanks, Alaska	$7.43	$9.86	$17.29
Atlanta, Georgia	$4.14	$10.55	$14.69
Seattle, Washington	$4.47	$9.95	$14.42
Boston, Massachusetts	$5.33	$6.62	$11.95
Birmingham, Alabama	$3.05	$7.96	$11.01
Portland, Oregon	$2.41	$8.51	$10.92
San Francisco, California	$1.97	$8.31	$10.28
Portland, Maine	$2.37	$7.66	$10.03
Austin, Texas	$3.84	$6.05	$9.89
Pittsburgh, Pennsylvania	$7.19	$2.27	$9.46
Chicago, Illinois	$4.81	$2.22	$7.03

Based on information from the Smart Energy Design Assistance Center, http://smartenergy.arch.uiuc.edu/.

6. Space heating and cooling
7. Domestic hot water
8. Lighting
9. Appliances
10. Renewable energy
11. Refrigerant management

Optimize Energy Performance

The "optimize energy performance" subcategory is centered on improving the overall energy efficiency of a home by meeting or exceeding the performance of an Energy Star-labeled home. As a minimum prerequisite, a LEED home must meet the performance requirements of Energy Star for Homes. As a result, any LEED-certified home is effectively also an Energy Star home.

After meeting this prerequisite, a home can receive credit–based on its Home Energy Rating System (HERS) index and climate zone–for going above and beyond the Energy Star requirements. Recall that the HERS Index is a comprehensive, whole-building analysis of a home's energy efficiency. It is a numerical value giving a picture of how the energy components of a home, such as insulation, air sealing, lighting, appliances, and any renewable energy systems, all interact together. The remaining energy and atmosphere subcategories present a list of design characteristics that can help a home achieve a low HERS index.

Insulation

The focus of the insulation subcategory is to design and install insulation to minimize heat transfer and thermal bridging. As a prerequisite, the insulation must meet or exceed the R-value requirements of the 2004 International Energy Conservation Code. The insulation must also be installed to meet the specifications of the Home Energy Ratings Standards and be verified by a rater conducting a thermal bypass inspection, which effectively is a pre-drywall inspection. A LEED home can gain additional credit if the insulation exceeds the minimum R-value standards by at least 5%.

Air Infiltration

The air infiltration subcategory is centered around minimizing energy consumption caused by uncontrolled air leakage into and out of conditioned spaces. The R-value of some insulation types, such as fiberglass, can be much lower than what its rated performance indicates if air infiltration is not properly addressed in design and construction. Homes must meet LEED minimum air leakage requirements and can gain additional credit for meeting requirements for greatly reduced or minimal energy leakage; this ensures the adequate sealing of the building's air envelope. Varying credits in this subcategory are based on tables of tested values.

Windows

The next area of focus is maximizing the energy performance of windows. The base requirement in this subcategory is for the windows to meet the requirements of the Energy Star for Homes national Builder Option Package. Homes can then gain credit for exceeding Energy Star requirements. To earn the label of "enhanced windows," Energy Star requirements must be exceeded by 10%. To earn the label of "exceptional windows," Energy Star requirements must be exceeded by 20%.

Duct Tightness

The next subcategory is centered on minimizing energy consumption due to thermal bridges or leaks in the heating and cooling distribution system. Credit is based on the amount of distributions losses of forced-air or hydronic (nonducted) systems. In a LEED home, the ducts are actually tested for leakage rates to ensure that they have been properly installed and sealed.

Space Heating and Cooling

The next subcategory is intended to reduce energy consumption associated with the heating and cooling system. To meet the prerequisite, heating, ventilation, and air conditioning (HVAC) equipment must be designed and sized according to the American Society of Heating, Refrigerating and Air-Conditioning Engineers' (ASHRAE) *Handbook of Fundamentals*, the requirements of the Energy Star Builder Option Package must be met, and an Energy Star-labeled programmable thermostat must be installed. Additional credit is available based on efficiency levels exceeding ASHRAE design, installation, and efficiency standards.

Domestic Hot Water

Credit in the water heating subcategory can be earned for using an efficient water heating system, such as a central manifold system for hot water distribution, as well as using efficient equipment such as a tankless or solar water heater. Credit points are awarded for efficient hot water distribution, pipe insulation (pipes must be insulated to an R-value of at least R-4), and domestic hot water equipment.

Lighting

According to the Energy Information Administration's *2005 Residential Energy Consumption Survey*, lighting accounts for about 25% of residential energy use.[7] The LEED for Homes rating system rewards strategies to reduce lighting energy use, such as using Energy Star light fixtures or compact fluorescent light (CFL) bulbs with four-pin bases rather than standard screw-in bases.

Appliances

Reducing appliance energy use is another focus of the LEED energy and atmosphere criteria. Credit is given for high-efficiency appliances that bear the Energy Star label and water-efficient clothes washers.

Renewable Energy

While not required for LEED certification, the use of renewable electric generation systems is encouraged and rewarded according to the specifications of the renewable energy subcategory. Using a renewable electric generation system, such as solar panels or wind turbines, reduces the consumption of nonrenewable energy sources. The points awarded for this credit vary based on the percentage of electrical load supplied by the renewable energy system.

Refrigerant Management

The last energy and atmosphere subcategory is centered around selecting and testing air-conditioning refrigerant to ensure performance and minimize contributions to ozone depletion and global warming. As a prerequisite, the home's air conditioning system must be properly charged to meet the maximum system efficiency. Credit is also given for the use of appropriate HVAC refrigerants. Different refrigerants have different global warming and/or ozone depletion potential. Using less harmful refrigerants results in receiving more LEED credit points.

Materials and Resources

The choice of building materials is important for sustainable building because of the extensive network of extraction, processing, and transportation required. With that in mind, LEED's materials and resources category has three components.

1. Material-efficient framing
2. Environmentally preferable products
3. Waste management

---

7. For more information, visit http://tonto.eia.doe.gov/.

Material-Efficient Framing

Good design decisions, particularly in the framing of homes, can significantly reduce the demand for framing materials. A project can save framing materials and reduce site waste and cost without changing the home design. The intent here is that surplus wood on the job site finds a way to be used in the framing.

The overall framing order waste factor must be limited to 10% or less as a prerequisite in this subcategory. Credit can then be obtained for the following:

- Prior to construction, creating detailed framing plans and accompanying architectural details for use on the job site
- Prior to construction, creating a detailed cut list and lumber order that corresponds directly to the framing plans
- Implementing framing-efficiency measures, such as using precut framing packages, structural insulated panes (SIPs), or advanced framing techniques (24" centers, ladder blocking, two-stud corners, etc.)
- Using panelized construction or modular, prefabricated construction as an alternative to on-site framing

Environmentally Preferable Products

The focus of the next materials and resources subcategory is on increasing demand for environmentally preferable products and products or building components that are extracted, processed, and manufactured within the region. As a prerequisite, any tropical wood must be certified by the Forest Stewardship Council (FSC), or a notice requesting FSC-certified tropical wood must be sent to all wood product suppliers. The FSC certifies woods that come from forest managers who adopt environmentally and socially responsible forest management practices (rather than clear-cutting forests) and companies that manufacture and sell products made from certified wood. These criteria have been established by the FSC to ensure the health and productivity of forests for timber production, wildlife habitat, clean air and water supplies, climate stabilization, and social benefits, such as community employment.[8] FSC lumber is not required for all wood used, such as framing lumber, but a project can earn points if it chooses to use FSC-certified wood.

Credit in this subcategory is given for the use of environmentally preferable products, which are those that contain certain percentages of recycled products, have low emissions, or are extracted, processed,

---

8. USGBC, *New Construction & Major Renovation Reference Guide.*

and manufactured within 500 miles of the home. Using locally produced items reduces the energy consumed in transporting materials to the site and the amount of greenhouse gasses emitted in the process. Building components such as countertops made from recycled glass, insulation made from recycled denim, and hardwood flooring reclaimed from another structure are a few examples of environmentally preferred products that can earn a project team points.

Waste Management

The waste management subcategory is centered around reducing waste generation to a level below the industry norm. According to the USGBC, www.usgbc.org, construction and demolition waste constitutes about 30% of the total solid waste stream in the United States. LEED's waste management prerequisite calls for investigating and documenting local options for the diversion of the project waste stream, such as the recycling and reuse of materials. It also requires documentation of the diversion rate for construction waste.

Credit in this subcategory is awarded for the reduction or diversion of waste generated from new construction activities to 2.5 pounds or less per square foot of conditioned floor area. Additional credit comes from diverting 25% or more of the total waste materials taken off the construction site from landfills and incinerators.

Indoor Environmental Quality

As mentioned in Chapter 1, Americans spend an average of 90% of their time indoors, where pollution levels typically run two to five times and occasionally more than 100 times higher than those outdoors. LEED's indoor environmental quality category focuses on improving this situation. This category is divided into the following ten subcategories:

1. Energy Star with IndoorPlus
2. Combustion venting
3. Moisture control
4. Outdoor air ventilation
5. Local exhaust
6. Distribution systems
7. Air filtering
8. Contaminant control
9. Radon protection
10. Vehicle emissions protection

As high-performance homes are built with energy-efficient construction methods, such as using improved insulation and preventing air infiltration, the home becomes a tighter structure. Without the natural air leakage that occurs in standard construction, this puts the occupants of the home at greater risk. The indoor environmental quality measures identified in LEED help minimize this risk, ensuring a healthy and comfortable home.

Energy Star with IndoorPlus

The Energy Star with IndoorPlus subcategory is centered on improving the overall quality of a home's indoor environment by installing an approved bundle of air quality measures. Projects that participate in the EPA's Energy Star with IndoorPlus initiative automatically qualify for points in this subcategory.

Combustion Venting

The aim of the next indoor environmental quality subcategory is to minimize the leakage of combustion gases into the occupied space of the home. As a prerequisite, the following basic combustion venting measures must be taken:

- No unvented combustion appliances, such as decorative logs, can be used
- A carbon monoxide monitor must be installed on each floor
- Fireplaces and wood stoves must have doors
- Combustion space and water heating equipment must have one of the following:
    - Closed combustion (sealed supply and exhaust ducting)
    - Power-vented exhaust
    - Location in a detached or open air building

These measures help prevent any combustion gases from contaminating the indoor air quality of the home. Credit is also given for enhanced combustion venting measures, which are defined by LEED as either 1) not installing a fireplace or woodstove, or 2) installing a fireplace or woodstove according to LEED specifications.

Moisture Control

The next subcategory has to do with controlling indoor moisture levels to provide comfort, reduce the risk of mold, and increase the home's durability. Having non-paper-based wall covering in shower surrounds and exhausting moist air from bathrooms and kitchens are requirements. Credit is given for installing dehumidification equipment to maintain relative humidity at or below 60%.

Outdoor Air Ventilation

The outdoor air ventilation subcategory focuses on reducing occupant exposure to indoor pollutants by ventilating with outdoor air to introduce fresh air to the otherwise stale indoor environment. The prerequisite in this category is to install a whole building ventilation system that complies with the ASHRAE residential standard for acceptable indoor air quality.

Credit can then be obtained for installing heat-recovery ventilators (HRVs) or energy-recovery ventilators (ERVs). According to Toolbase Services of the NAHB Research Center, www.toolbase.org, an HRV can help make mechanical ventilation more cost effective by reclaiming energy from exhaust airflows. HRVs use heat exchangers to heat or cool incoming fresh air, recapturing 60% to 80% of the conditioned temperatures that would otherwise be lost. ERVs, on the other hand, are models that exchange moisture in addition to energy between the two air streams. According to the EPA, www.epa.gov, ERVs provide a controlled way of ventilating a home while minimizing energy loss. They reduce the costs of heating ventilated air in the winter by transferring heat from the warm inside air being exhausted to the fresh, cold supply air. In the summer, the inside air cools the warmer supply air to reduce ventilation cooling costs. ERVs are more common in cold climates as HRVs that do not exchange moisture can run into ice buildup on the exhaust ports.

Local Exhaust

The local exhaust subcategory focuses on reducing moisture and exposure to indoor pollutants in kitchens and bathrooms. The prerequisite for this subcategory is that projects must be designed and installed to meet the ASHRAE standard for kitchen and bath exhaust. Credit can then be obtained for the installation of such features as an occupancy sensor, automatic humidistat controller, or automatic timer. Buildings with an ERV or HRV can often use these devices as a central exhaust fan for bathrooms. Credit is also available for third-party testing of the exhaust air flow rate out of the home to ensure that ducts have been installed and perform properly.

Distribution Systems

The next subcategory covers the distribution of space heating and cooling for forced air systems to improve the thermal comfort and energy performance of the home. Credits are broken down based on the type of HVAC system used.

For forced air systems, performing design calculations and installing ducts accordingly is a prerequisite. Credit can be obtained for having supply air flow rates tested by a third party and ensuring that rooms have adequate return flows of replacement air.

For hydronic (nonducted) systems, performing room-by-room load calculations and installing systems accordingly is a prerequisite. Credit is given for installing 1) flow control valves on each radiator or baseboard convector, or 2) a nonducted HVAC system with at least two distinct zones with independent thermostats.

Builders may face a bit of a learning curve with this area, as HVAC ducts are tested for air leakage rates. The traditional sealing of seams with duct tape may not be sufficient, and the installer may need to use mastic adhesive.

Air Filtering

Reducing particulate matter from the air supply system improves the indoor air quality in a home. Air filters are measured using a minimum efficiency reporting value (MERV) rating. The higher the rating, the more particulates removed from the air. Installing air filters with a MERV rating of at least 8 is a prerequisite in this subcategory. Credit is given for installing air filters with higher MERV ratings. Filtration equipment, such as UV lamps or ozone filters with no filtration media, has no MERV rating and cannot meet the requirements of this credit on its own. However, it may be installed in addition to a MERV-rated filter.

Contaminant Control

The next subcategory focuses on reducing occupants' and construction workers' exposure to indoor airborne contaminants through source control and removal. Sealing all permanent ducts and vents to minimize contamination during construction is a prerequisite. Credit is available for features such as permanent walk-off mats, shoe removal and storage areas, and central vacuum systems with exhausts to the outside. Credit is also available for flushing the entire home with fresh air for 48 hours before occupancy, keeping windows open, running a fan, and replacing or cleaning HVAC air filters.

Radon Protection

This subcategory seeks to reduce occupant exposure to radon, a cancer-causing natural radioactive gas, and other soil gas contaminants. Radon is produced by uranium-bearing rocks in the soil. Credit in this subcategory is awarded based on the home's location. The prerequisite is to design and build the home with radon-resistant construction techniques as prescribed by the EPA or an equivalent standard if the home is located within a region that the EPA has designated as high risk. Connecticut, Maine, Massachusetts, New Hampshire, Rhode Island, and Vermont are designated as high-risk areas. Credit is given for designing and building a home with radon-resistant construction techniques as prescribed by the EPA or an equivalent standard if the home is located outside of a designated high-risk area.

Vehicle Emissions Protection

The final indoor air quality subcategory is focused on reducing occupant exposure to indoor pollutants originating from a home's adjacent garage. Alternatively, a home may have a detached garage or no garage and receive extra points. If an attached garage is in the home's design, it is a prerequisite that no HVAC should be present in the garage. Credit is given for tightly sealing all shared surfaces between the garage and conditioned spaces as well as installing an exhaust fan in the garage that is rated for continuous operation.

Awareness and Education

Most of the LEED for Homes Rating System addresses the design and construction of green homes, but the environmental impact of a home continues throughout its life cycle of use by the homeowners or tenants. The awareness and education category is centered around maintaining the performance of the home by providing education about the operations and maintenance of the home's LEED features and equipment. This category is divided into two subcategories.

- Education of the homeowner or tenant
- Education of the building manager

Education of the Homeowner or Tenant

As a prerequisite in the "education of the homeowner or tenant" subcategory, occupants must be provided with guidance on occupant activities as well as an operations and maintenance manual for the home and its equipment. There also must be a minimum one-hour walk-through of the home with the occupant to identify equipment and discuss how to operate and maintain it. Credit can be earned by providing additional training and promoting a general awareness of LEED for Homes by conducting public open houses, creating a Web site, generating newspaper coverage, or erecting signage on the property.

Education of the Building Manager

This subcategory is limited to homes of more than five residential units. Credit can be earned by educating the building manager about the operation and maintenance of the home's LEED features and equipment.

LEED for Homes Providers

Because the LEED for Homes Rating System is relatively new and requires local implementation support, the USGBC has instituted a network of LEED for Homes providers. Providers are local organizations with demonstrated local knowledge and expertise. Their functions are

- Marketing the LEED program to local builders
- Providing rating support services to builders
- Training, coordinating, and overseeing LEED-qualified inspectors and builder support staff

These providers are the project team's main point of contact and provide the third-party verification services critical for LEED certification. Exhibit 3.7 shows the locations of LEED for Homes providers as of 2010.[9]

Exhibit 3.7 Locations of LEED for Homes Providers

Based on information provided by the USGBC, www.usgbc.org.

9. Visit the USGBC's Web site at www.usgbc.org for the most recent version of this map. Click on "LEED" in the upper left corner of the home page. Next, click on "LEED Rating Systems," then "Homes," and then "Providers." The direct link is http://www.usgbc.org/DisplayPage.aspx?CMSPageID=1554/.

Economic Benefits

LEED-certified homes enjoy some economic benefits. For example, some home insurance companies, such as Farmers' Insurance and Fireman's Fund, offer 5% insurance premium discounts for homes that have been LEED-certified by a third party. The lower risk incurred by the insurer is a reflection of the increased durability inspections and verification a LEED home undergoes. Also, some lenders are now beginning to offer discounted mortgage rates for LEED-certified homes. One national lender, Prospect Mortgage, offers 25 to 100 points off the borrower's interest rate depending on the home's LEED certification status–a "certified" home earns 25 points off, a "silver" home earns 50 points off, a "gold" home earns 75 points off, and a "platinum" home earns 100 points off.

Further incentives are available in local municipalities. For example, the city of Cincinnati offers a tax abatement program for LEED-certified buildings in which the construction of one-, two-, and three-unit residential structures (including condominiums) are eligible for a 15-year 100% tax abatement, valued at up to $500,000.[10] Other municipalities such as Northbrook, Illinois, offer construction permit rebates based on the building's LEED certification level–10% for "certified" buildings, 20% for "silver," 30%" for "gold," and 40% for "platinum."[11]

International Green Construction Code

In March of 2010, the International Green Construction Code (IGCC) was launched by the ICC, the ASHRAE, the USGBC, and the Illuminating Engineering Society of North America (IES). This code represents a combination of national efforts to develop adoptable and enforceable green commercial building codes and is a significant development in the buildings industry. While the code establishes a regulatory framework for the construction of green commercial buildings, it is likely to encourage an increase in all types of green building across the United States.

---

10. For more information, visit http://www.cincinnati-oh.gov/cdap/pages/-3521-/.
11. For more information, visit http://www.northbrook.il.us/Services/Green/green%20 build.pdf.

1327 W. Magnolia

The first home in Colorado to achieve a LEED "silver" rating provides a good example of various green building attributes. This home is located at 1327 W. Magnolia in Fort Collins, Colorado.

At first glance, this home looks quite similar to most new homes. However, special design features of this residence make it a sustainable, high-performance home.

The house at 1327 W. Magnolia in Fort Collins, Colorado. Photo appears courtesy of Joe Sullivan, President, Archer Homes, Inc.

The ICF foundation being put in place. Photo appears courtesy of Joe Sullivan, President, Archer Homes, Inc.

Insulating Concrete Form Foundation

Insulating concrete forms (ICFs) are rigid plastic foam forms, similar to Lego blocks, that hold concrete in place during curing and remain in place afterward to serve as thermal insulation. They come in lightweight sections and are joined together on site. Typical insulation values range from R-17 to R-26 for the completed walls, compared to between R-13 and R-19 for most wood-framed walls. Exterior sheathing and interior wallboard can be screwed directly to supports embedded in the foam.

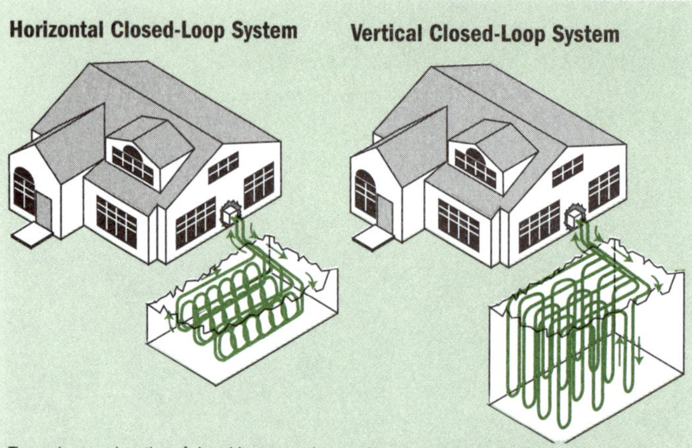

The underground portion of closed-loop ground source heat pumps, much like the system used at 1327 W. Magnolia. Source: U.S. Department of Energy's Energy Savers Web site, www.energysavers.gov.

This photo shows the ground source heat pump in the basement of 1327 W. Magnolia. Photo appears courtesy of Joe Sullivan, President, Archer Homes, Inc.

Ground Source Heat Pumps with Radiant Floor Heating

The homeowners of 1327 W. Magnolia narrowed down the list of heating options to six alternatives, and these were modeled and distributed for bidding. The ideal system was chosen based on comfort, payback, and other considerations. The owners ended up selecting a ground source heat pump (also known as a *geothermal heat pump*) to heat and cool the building.

Geothermal technology relies on the earth's natural heat. Vertically drilled holes or horizontal trenches pull heat up through loops of liquid-filled pipe generated through a heat pump and distributed throughout the house in a constant cyclical action. During the summer this works like an air conditioner, except that instead of putting the heat into the atmosphere using a condenser, it uses the earth as a heat sink. During the winter, it works in reverse by extracting heat from the earth. Using the relatively constant temperature of the earth to heat and cool homes and businesses allows geothermal heat pumps to run on 40% to 70% less energy than conventional systems. A geothermal heat pump can move up to four units of heat for every unit of electricity needed to power the system, resulting in a practical equivalence of over 400% efficiency.

When compared to a forced-air system, the radiant floor heating system makes the whole floor warmer, radiates more heat, and retains the heat for longer periods of time. Photo appears courtesy of Joe Sullivan, President, Archer Homes, Inc.

In this particular home, the radiant heating system installed in the floor is very efficient. This system uses coils of pipes embedded in the floor. The whole floor gets warmer, radiates more warmth, and retains the heat for longer periods of time as compared to a forced-air system.

Soy-Based Polyurethane Insulation

The house at 1327 W. Magnolia also features soy-based polyurethane insulation, providing R-values of R-35 for the walls and R-56 for the ceilings. Spray-foam insulation has been around for several years, but companies have recently begun to produce polyurethane insulation made from soybean oil instead of petroleum-based oil. When sprayed on, this foam

- Expands to 100 times its original size
- Fills all cracks and crevices
- Reduces air infiltration
- Reduces noise infiltration
- Reduces allergic reactions
- Will not support mold growth, rodents, or insects
- Will not sag or settle

Spray-foam polyurethane insulation made from soybean oil.

Because of the product's composition, it contributes toward LEED for Homes credit in the energy and atmosphere category (for optimizing energy performance), in the materials and resources category (for being rapidly renewable), and in the indoor environmental quality category (for helping to control pollutant infiltration). Brand names for this type of insulation include Bio-Based, Dow's Great Stuff, and Emega.

Other Features

Additional features of the Colorado house are listed below and their placement within the LEED for Homes rating system is indicated.

- Solar photovoltaic panels (energy and atmosphere)
- Energy-efficient lighting and Energy Star features throughout (energy and atmosphere)
- Air-tight construction and exhaust-only air quality system with heat recovery system (indoor environmental quality)
- Recycled plastic deck material (materials and resources)
- On-site waste reduction and recycling practices (materials and resources)
- Environmentally preferable building materials and flooring (materials and resources)
- Low-flow water fixtures (water efficiency)

- A xeriscaped yard, which uses a variety of native and weather-tolerant plants in order to save water (sustainable sites, water efficiency)
- Building diagnostics and performance test (energy and atmosphere)

Many factors in this home should have an impact on its value. It is well sealed and insulated to make it comfortable and to promote good indoor air quality. Water efficiency, solar panels, a geothermal heating and cooling system, and energy-efficient lighting all result in dramatically lower energy bills compared to a house of conventional construction. This home was also constructed to a higher quality level with its soy-based polyurethane insulation and ICF foundation.

Five other case studies from the USGBC appear in Appendix E in the back of this book. Three of the featured properties in the Appendix are single-unit homes and two are affordable housing projects; even affordable housing projects are now being built green and LEED certified. The reduced utility costs of green affordable housing provides a major benefit, while the improved indoor environmental quality of green housing provides healthier places to live. Additional project profiles can be found at www.usgbc.org; the direct link is http://www.usgbc.org/DisplayPage.aspx?CMSPageID=1721/.

CHAPTER 4

Green Building Products

It can be difficult to pin down exactly what a green building product is. "Green" is a label that many people use indiscriminately and hope for instant cachet. Anything that is labeled "green" may prove to be a hot commodity, and it has become a marketer's catchphrase. Green cars, green cleaning products, green computers, and green houses are all being advertised and marketed today.

Building Green, Inc., Products

Many product certifications have evolved to identify truly "green" building and consumer products. For example, Building Green, Inc., describes itself at www.buildinggreen.com as an independent company committed to providing accurate, unbiased, and timely information to help building industry professionals and policy makers improve the environmental performance and reduce the adverse impact of buildings. Building Green publishes the *Environmental Building News* newsletter and the *GreenSpec Directory*, which lists product descriptions for over 2,100 environmentally preferable products. Listings and information on environmentally friendly products are also available online for a fee.

In his article "Building Materials: What Makes a Product Green?" Alex Wilson explains the difficulties of defining a "green" product.

> Very often, we are comparing apples to oranges. We are trying to weigh, for example, the resource-extraction impacts of one product with the manufacturing impacts of another, and the indoor air-quality impacts of a third. Even in the greenest of projects it is likely that many products will be used that are not themselves green–but they are used in a manner that helps reduce the overall environmental impacts of the building. A particular window may not be green, but the way it is used maximizes collection of low winter sunlight and blocks the summer sun.

> It is important also to note that multiple criteria often apply–in other words, a product may be considered green for more than one reason. Take recycled plastic lumber, for example: it's made from recycled waste, it's highly durable, and it can obviate the need for pesticide treatments.[1]

Environmentally friendly products that appear in the *GreenSpec Directory* or in Building Green's online database must meet at least one of the following criteria:

- Contain salvaged, recycled, or agricultural waste materials
- Conserve natural resources
- Avoid toxic or other emissions
- Save energy or water
- Contribute to a safe and healthy environment

The first two criteria will be examined more closely in the following discussion.

Products Made with Salvaged, Recycled, or Agricultural Waste Content

Salvaged materials save on raw material use and reduce energy costs for manufacture and transportation. Some materials can be salvaged on site and others can be bought from salvage yards. Examples of salvaged materials include bricks, beams, framing lumber, period hardware, plumbing fixtures, and doors.

The term *post-consumer material* is used to describe waste material that is generated by end users and that can no longer be used for its intended purpose. Examples of post-consumer materials include concrete recycled from demolition debris, recycled deck material, carpet fibers made from recycled plastic soda bottles, and rubber flooring made from recycled tires.

The term *pre-consumer material* is used to define waste material that has been diverted from the waste stream during the manufacturing process. Examples of pre-consumer materials include products made wholly or partially from sawdust, wood chips, wood shavings, print overruns, or fabric scraps.

Products that Conserve Natural Resources

Products that conserve natural resources can be broken down into the following subcategories:

- Products that reduce material use

---

1. Alex Wilson, Building Green, Inc. "Building Materials: What Makes a Product Green?," www.buildinggreen.com (January 2006). Direct link: http://www.buildinggreen.com/auth/article.cfm?fileName=090101a.xml/.

- Certified wood products
- Rapidly renewable products
- Products that have exceptional durability or low-maintenance requirements

Certified wood products, such as wood certified by the Forest Stewardship Council (FSC), have been discussed in Chapter 3.

Rapidly renewable products have a short harvest time of typically 10 years or less. Examples of rapidly renewable products include bamboo floors, cork floors, cotton insulation, wool carpeting, wheatboard cabinets, and soy-based building products.

Products that have exceptional durability last a long time and require little or no maintenance. Examples of such products include fiber-cement siding, fiberglass windows, slate shingles, and deck products that are made from reclaimed or recycled materials (such as Trex deck products).

A quick Internet search of the phrase "green building product" produces over 127 million hits. This search can be narrowed considerably by specifying the green items desired, such as decking, flooring, insulation, windows, or plumbing fixtures. Web sites that list and describe multiple green building products for sale can be found in the list of green building online resources in Appendix A at the back of this book.

Top Energy Savers

The top five energy-efficient home building products and measures, as listed by the National Association of Home Builders (NAHB), www.nahb.org, are compact fluorescent lighting, programmable thermostats, tree conservation, high-performance windows, and Energy Star appliances.

Compact Fluorescent Lighting

One of the easiest things that can be done to save energy in the home is to replace conventional light bulbs with compact fluorescent lighting (CFL). It is best to switch out incandescent bulbs with CFLs in areas that are usually lit for at least two hours at a time, because switching a CFL on and off too frequently shortens its life.

CFLs use 50%-80% less energy and last up to 10 times longer than conventional incandescent bulbs. While typical incandescent bulbs have an average lifetime of 750 to 2,500 hours, CFLs last 6,000 to 10,000 hours. CFL bulbs range from $4 to $15, depending on their type. While CFL bulbs are more expensive than typical incandescent bulbs, the energy bill savings and fewer number of bulbs to replace over time make up for this extra cost.

Programmable Thermostats

Programmable thermostats can be installed to set heating and cooling equipment to automatically turn on or off to match a schedule and create a comfortable and energy-efficient living environment. These units typically offer savings of 10%-15% and cost $40 to $100. Setting the thermostat to a higher temperature in the summer and a cooler temperature in the winter–especially during times when no one is home–results in even more savings.

Tree Conservation

Properly placed trees and shrubs can help reduce utility bills. Tree preservation reduces landscaping and future energy costs and helps provide winter wind breaks or summer shade. Deciduous trees planted on the west and south sides of a home help to keep the house shaded during the day's peak heating times. Plus, as an added benefit, one tree can filter 60 pounds of pollutants from the air each year.

High-Performance Windows

Double-pane windows with high-performance (i.e., low emissivity or "low-E") glass that are gas-filled perform much better than single-pane windows and help reduce heat loss in the winter and heat gain in the summer. Low-E coatings save energy in most U.S. climates. Low-E coatings used to add about $1 per square foot of glazing. However, this has now become the standard in most climates. Interior storm windows provide a compromise by increasing energy efficiency while maintaining exterior aesthetics at a significant cost savings over window replacement.

Energy Star Appliances

Energy Star-rated appliances are designed to use 10%-50% less energy and water than standard appliances and save money at an average of 30% over standard models. The up-front costs of these appliances are usually higher, but the payback over time makes up for the extra costs. The Energy Star label can be found on products such as induction cooktops, high-efficiency refrigerators, and front-loading clothes washers.

Induction Cooktops

Rather than heating the cooking surfaces, the magnetic induction process in induction cooktops turns the pot into the heating element. As a result, food is heated more quickly and to more precise temperatures. Cooking with magnetic induction is 90% efficient, as compared to approximately 65% efficiency in resistance electric cooktops and approximately 55% efficiency in open-flamed gas cooktops. A magnetic induction cooktop costs three to four times more than an electric cooktop. A magnetic induction cooktop with four elements ranges in price from $1,800 to $4,000, depending on the manufacturer and features.

High-Efficiency Refrigerators

Refrigerators are one of the top energy consumers out of all household appliances. As a result, federal regulations have mandated energy ratings and efficiency improvements for all refrigerators. New high-efficiency refrigerators exceed the federal energy requirements and can save consumers a substantial amount of money. Today's generation of refrigerators feature more insulation, high-efficiency compressors, better door seals, and more accurate control of temperature than what is found in older models. A modern 15-cubic-foot, top-freezer refrigerator model uses about 450 kilowatt-hours (kWh) of electricity per year, while similar models in the recent past used about 700 kWh of electricity per year. A typical 1973 model used nearly three times as much electrical energy as a similar model today. Furthermore, refrigerators certified by the Energy Star program must yield a minimum 15% improvement over the federal standard. Replacing a 10-year-old refrigerator with a new, high-efficiency refrigerator can save a homeowner $100 in average annual energy costs, assuming a national average energy cost of $0.084 per kWh.

Front-Loading Clothes Washers

While the Energy Star label can be found on both top-loading and front-loading washers, front-loading washers use less water, energy, and detergent overall. According to the EPA, www.epa.gov, front-loading washing machines can use about 40% less water and 50% less energy than conventional washers, cause less wear and tear on clothes, and accommodate larger items. A typical top-loading washer uses about 40 gallons of water per full load. In contrast, a full-sized, front-loading clothes washer uses between 20 and 25 gallons of water. Front-loading washers cost between $600 and $1,500, which is more expensive than top-loading machines. However, the estimated annual utility bill savings for a family of four using a front-loading clothes washer is about $75 to $100, plus any additional savings associated with shorter drying time and reduced detergent use.

The next section of this chapter will focus on some of the newer or more unusual green products that one may encounter when appraising a sustainable residential property.

Green Home Design Considerations

Stormwater Runoff Control

One of the major concerns in site design is the control of stormwater. When it rains, the amount of water runoff needs to be controlled. Controlling stormwater runoff is important for the following reasons:

- It is desirable to retain much, if not most, of the stormwater. Stormwater is free and can be used for landscape irrigation. It can also be reclaimed for nonpotable use in toilet and urinal flushing or for custodial use. Stormwater may be collected in cisterns or rain barrels and stored for future use. It may also be stored in bioswales or retention ponds and used for fire control in certain areas.
- Unused water can be infiltrated into the ground to recharge local aquifers.
- Unwanted runoff can endanger neighboring properties and create flooding situations.
- Controlling stormwater runoff reduces the load on storm sewers and prevents the clogging and silting of systems.
- Controlling runoff helps prevent erosion and loss of topsoil.

A storage container for stormwater runoff. Photo appears courtesy of www.humphrey-house.com.

The most effective way to reduce stormwater runoff is to reduce the amount of impervious, or impermeable, area on a site. This can be accomplished through measures such as

- Using pervious (permeable) paving materials
- Installing green roofs

- Creating smaller building footprints
- Reducing the amount of paved surfaces (roads, sidewalks, patios, etc.)

Pervious Paving Materials

Pervious paving materials help with stormwater runoff and also combat urban heat island effect. Pervious paving materials can be made from concrete. Some concrete is made so that water can seep through it and back into the ground. This type of concrete employs little or no sand and 15%-25% of the concrete is "void" with air spaces, yet it is still strong and can support the weight of traditional concrete.

Pervious pavers are installed above a reservoir of aggregate such as crushed stone or gravel with a layer of landscape cloth underneath. Pervious pavers are fine for driveways and walkways but may break down in heavily trafficked areas under heavy loads. They require periodic cleaning with a pressure washer or blower, as dirt can clog the holes and prevent drainage. Pervious asphalt has also been developed. It is made with coarser materials and allows drainage to a bed of gravel underneath.

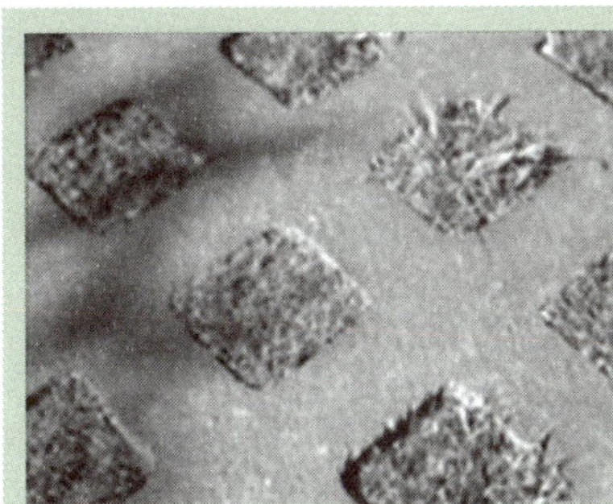

Plantable paving material, in which stone alternates with grass, is better at absorbing water than conventional paving material. Photo appears courtesy of Pavestone Company.

Perforated concrete building blocks were first used in Germany in 1961 for overflow parking. Some products use concrete paving stones that are honeycombed and filled with gravel, which allows water to filter through the voids. Plantable pavers, in which paving stones alternate with grass- or gravel-filled areas, are also available. A new type of pervious paving product is Ekopaver, which is made of a ceramic material and allows water to drain directly through it.

Ekopaver material is made of ceramic and allows water to drain directly through it. Photo appears courtesy of Airostone Corp.

Vegetated Roofs

Vegetated roofs, also known as "green roofs," have been used on commercial and industrial roofs in Europe for over 25 years. Over 20 million square feet of vegetated roof cover can now be found in Germany alone. Vegetated roofs are less common in residential applications, but this is changing.

Vegetated roofs are beneficial because they

- Control stormwater runoff
- Produce a cooling effect
- Provide good insulation
- Improve air quality
- Have aesthetic appeal

The typical vegetated roof system consists of various layered components such as

- A roof deck
- A moisture barrier
- Insulation
- A drainage layer that usually consists of aggregates such as pea gravel
- A root barrier
- Separation fabric
- A growing medium

Various sources cite the range of costs for vegetated roofs as $9 to $24 per square foot. Of course, this varies based on the design of the roof and its total size. Economies of scale may be encountered in larger installations.

EPA Demonstration Roof

The EPA installed an approximately 3,000-sq.-ft. demonstration garden on the roof of the Fencing Academy of Philadelphia. The plants in this demonstration roof system

- Capture and hold precipitation in the foliage
- Absorb water in the root zone
- Slow the velocity of runoff
- Cool the temperature of the air and the runoff

This demonstration roof has been monitored to measure runoff control, and it has worked very well. The roof consists of three layers:

1. A synthetic under-drain layer that promotes the rapid drainage of water from the surface of the roof deck
2. Thin, lightweight growth media that permit installation on existing conventional roofs

3. A setting of sedum plant varieties, which do not need irrigation or regular maintenance

These components of the vegetated roof cover are illustrated in Exhibit 4.1.

Vegetated roof systems usually have greater weight, and the roof structure must be designed to accommodate this. According to the EPA, the demonstration roof weighs about five pounds per square foot when dry and 17 pounds per square foot when saturated. However, during the spring and summer, temperatures on a neighboring black tar roof varied by as much as 90°F, while the variation under the demonstration 2.74-inch vegetated cover was only 18°F. This vegetated cover also insulates the roof in winter and protects the roof membrane from the elements. Vegetated rooftop covers can potentially extend the life of a roof by 20 years or more.

Exhibit 4.1 Vegetated Roof Cover Layers

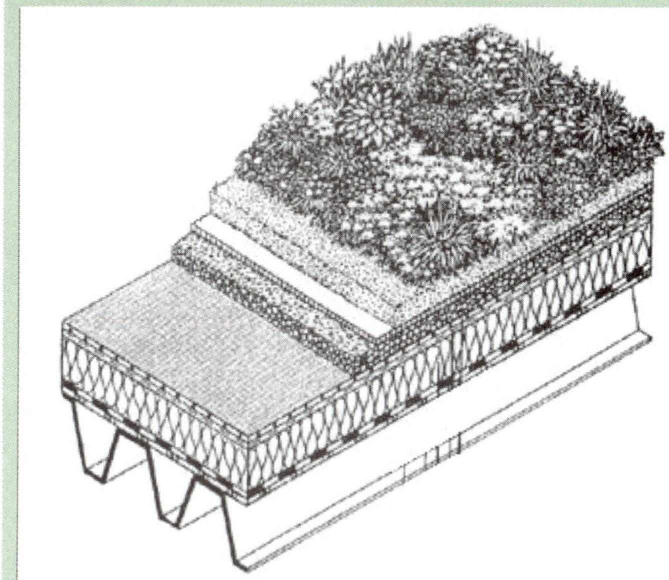

Source: EPA project report on vegetated roof cover, Philadelphia, Pennsylvania. Available at www.epa.gov. Direct link: http://www.epa.gov/owow/nps/roofcover.pdf/.

One of the first green roofs in North America was installed on top of Chicago's City Hall building in 2000. Photo source: Roofscapes, Inc. Photo appears courtesy of GreenRoofs.com.

Vegetated Roofs in Chicago

Chicago has earned a reputation as the "greenest city in

America" and has won several awards from the Green Roofs for Healthy Cities (GRHC) organization for having more square footage of green roofs than any other city in the United States. Chicago mayor Richard M. Daley started this effort in 2000 when he had one of the first green roofs in North America installed on top of Chicago's City Hall building.

Chicago has instituted programs for financial assistance, grants, and expedited permitting for green roofs on new commercial, small commercial (less than 10,000 square feet), and residential properties. The city also has grant programs encouraging green roof installations on existing buildings in the downtown area. So far, over four million square feet of vegetated roofs have been installed on more than 250 buildings in Chicago.

Insulation

Spray-foam polyurethane insulation was discussed in Chapter 3. While blanket insulation still has many applications, newer and more sustainable insulation materials are becoming available. Fiberglass blanket insulation (in rolls) has been used for at least 30 years and is made of silica spun into glass fibers with a phenol-formaldehyde binder. Formaldehyde-free fiberglass products have become available in recent years, and most fiberglass insulation today is made with 30%-40% recycled glass content.

New innovations have also been made recently for insulation that uses natural products such as wool, cotton, hay, and straw. When these renewable materials are treated with fire-resistant borates, the result is a compelling alternative to fiberglass. Cotton insulation is made from recycled cotton textiles, such as denim, with synthetic fibers added to maintain loft. Nontoxic fire retardants are also added. Cotton insulation does not contain mineral microfibers, which may cause respiratory problems. Wool insulation products are made from natural wool plus natural latex and a borax solution. Borax, a natural salt, is a pest-repellent and adds to the fire protection rating of the insulation. Wool can also absorb formaldehyde emitted by other building products.

Loose-fill insulation, such as cellulose, also has some applications. Recycled newspaper makes up 75%-80% of most loose-fill insulations. Nontoxic borax is also added to the insulation as a fire retardant. Cellulose can also be blown into existing walls, making it an attractive insulation choice in existing construction and remodeling.

Building Envelope Technologies

Although insulation covers most of the building envelope, some other technologies are being used to help control energy performance in the thermal envelope, such as fiberglass windows and steel.

Fiberglass Windows

Fiberglass window frames are stronger than aluminum, vinyl, or wood frames. When filled with insulation, they provide better thermal breaks and reduce heat loss. Fiberglass does not warp or crack, and it is a natural insulator that does not conduct heat or cold. It requires no maintenance or painting. Fiberglass is made from silica sand and is nontoxic.

Steel

Steel also has environmental attributes, although many people would not initially think this is so. Steel's initial production may consume a lot of energy, but much of the steel used today contains 30%-95% recycled content. At the end of their usual lives, approximately 90% of steel products are recycled into new products. Steel is obviously strong, durable, and fire-resistant. It may be found in residential applications including beams, columns, studs, doors, and siding. Steel's use as a roofing material has also increased.

Interior Finishes

A variety of green products can also be used inside the home.

Paints and Caulking

Many products that contain little or no volatile organic compounds (VOCs) have recently become available. These products include low-VOC or zero-VOC interior paints, primers, sealants, and caulking. Ordinary paints and primers can be serious culprits of *off-gassing*, meaning that they gradually release gas that can cause respiratory and allergic reactions. Low-VOC content is usually classified as 50 grams or less per liter of VOCs for flat paints and 150 grams per liter for non-flat paints.

Green Seal, an independent nonprofit organization that promotes the manufacture and sale of environmentally responsible products, has created an environmental standard for paints and coatings known as GS-11. More information is available at www.greenseal.org.

Low-VOC stains are also becoming available. VOC content is posted on the labels. Generally, water-based stains have a much lower VOC content than oil-based stains.

Flooring and Floor Coverings

Flooring typically has an underlayment and a finish layer. Backing boards and underlayments made of environmentally preferable products such as cork, strawboard, and fiberboard based on recycled paper are now available. The adhesives used to install these floor coverings are also important.

Finished flooring products can be made of green materials such as

- Cork
- Bamboo
- Recycled carpet
- FSC-certified wood
- Recycled glass tile
- Reclaimed wood
- Linoleum

Cork

Cork is peeled from the outer bark of the cork oak tree and has been used for over 200 years. It regenerates in about 10 years and some cork oaks can be continuously harvested for up to 200 years. It is durable, hypoallergenic, sound absorbent, and resistant to moisture, fire, and mold.

Bamboo

Bamboo has a quick growth rate and is easily sustainable. Most bamboo used around the world comes from bamboo trees in China. The bamboo tree matures in three years. When the tree matures, only the stalks are cut off and the roots are left to regenerate. In addition to its rapid regeneration, bamboo is beneficial because it is durable, hard, and processed without preservatives. A negative feature of bamboo is that most bamboo flooring is glued together with urea-formaldehyde, a VOC. However, some new glue products are being made free of formaldehyde.

Linoleum

Linoleum is a natural product made from linseed oil, pine rosin, sawdust, cork dust, limestone, natural pigments, and jute backing. It has none of the petroleum-based products or chlorinated chemicals that are found in vinyl flooring. Linoleum was originally popular in the 1950s and 1960s, but it grew out of favor when no-wax vinyl floors became available. Many people thought that linoleum was ugly, but it is a long-lasting material. Some linoleum floors from the 1950s and 1960s are still in use today. Linoleum is now available in bright colors and has once again become a hot item.

Flooring Adhesives

Flooring adhesives can be a major contributor to indoor air pollution. Many adhesives emit VOCs such as formaldehyde. Some air quality regulations restrict the manufacture, sale, and installation of adhesives that contain more than 150 grams of VOCs per liter. Many newer products are labeled as having low- or zero-VOC content, while others are water-based or made from natural materials.

Water Heaters

Gas or electric water heaters are one of the top energy-users in a home; they are second only to heating and cooling systems. Water heaters are typically responsible for 10% to 25% of the energy used in the home. A standard electric water heater also emits almost half as much carbon dioxide emissions as an automobile.

Heat Pump Water Heaters

Heat pump water heaters have been available for a while but are not widely used. They work on the same principles as heat pumps used for heating and air conditioning and employ a compressor and condenser. Heat pump water heaters are two to three times more efficient than conventional electric water heaters and work best in a space that has excess heat, such as a furnace room.

Tankless Water Heaters

On-demand water heaters are tankless and heat water only when needed. They are built into the water supply lines and have no storage tanks that need to keep water heated. Tankless water heaters can be gas- or electric-fired. Electric-fired models offer a 10%-20% water heating savings, while gas-fired models can save about 20%-40%. The equipment life of tankless water heaters may be longer than tank-type heaters because they are less subject to corrosion; a typical tankless water heater lasts approximately 20 years compared to a typical life span of 10 to 15 years for tank-type water heaters. Most gas models have sealed combustion chambers and no pilot lights. Tankless water heaters have been popular in Europe and Japan for a number of years because of their greater efficiency and smaller size. They are also frequently used as a backup water heating source in homes with solar-powered water heaters.

A tankless water heater, which heats water on an on-demand basis. Photo appears courtesy of www.humphrey-house.com.

Some on-demand heaters are used for whole-house water heating and some smaller units are used for individual bathrooms or hot tubs. They may also be used as boosters for dishwashers or washing machines.

According to *The Wall Street Journal's* article "The Green House Effect: Eco-Conscious Homes," a tankless water heater cost $585 to install in a Dallas home as compared to a cost of $188 for a standard tank-type model. However, the tankless heater uses 730 kWh less electricity annually than the tank model. This results in a power savings of $58 per year under local raters, which makes for a payback on the investment within 6.8 years.[2]

Reflective Roofs

Another way to save on energy is to keep attics cooler. The sun's rays heat up attics, and it takes energy to cool the interiors of homes to combat the attic heat that infiltrates. Color is also part of this equation; white roofs reflect more heat than black roofs.

Roofs absorb heat energy directly from the rays of the sun. Some energy is transferred inside and some is transferred out to add to the heat island effect in the atmosphere. When an object is warmed, it heats the air around it through the process of convection.

A recent technology known as the "cool roof" reflects away much of the solar energy. As a result, the roofs stay cooler (which adds to their life span), attics stay cooler, and the heat island effect is reduced.

The sun's energy arrives as short-wave radiation. When it is absorbed by an object, it is converted into a different form of energy and emits long-wave radiation. This has a warming effect, such as the energy given off by a wood stove or flooring heated by a radiant heating system. The amount of solar energy that may be deflected by a roof and sent back into the atmosphere is a function of the reflectance or emissivity of the roof's surface. Cool roofs are those with high reflectance and high emissivity.

As mentioned in Chapter 3, solar reflectance (also called *albedo*) is measured on a scale called the solar reflective index (SRI), for which a standard black surface has an SRI of 0% and a standard white surface has an SRI of 100%. *Emissivity* is the ratio of the radiation emitted by a surface to the amount of radiation emitted by a black surface at the same temperature. Cool roofs generally are defined by various authorities as having a reflectivity in the range of 65% to 70% and an emissivity of 75% to 80%. The amount of reflectance and emissivity is impacted not just by color, finish, texture, and substrate, but also by whether a roof is painted or not.

Metal roofing is energy efficient, durable (lasts 30 years or more), sustainable (can be 100% recycled at the end of its life), and fire- and wind-resistant. When a steel roof is properly installed and insulated, noise and vibration concerns are alleviated.

---

2. James Carlton, "The Green House Effect: Eco-Conscious Homes," *The Wall Street Journal* (2007), http://online.wsj.com/.

Radiant Roof Barriers

On a sunny summer day, solar energy is absorbed by the roof, heating the roof sheathing and causing the underside of the sheathing and roof framing to radiate heat downward toward the attic floor. Radiant roof barriers may be applied to roof sheathing to further reduce heat gain in attics. This type of barrier can be a layer of aluminum integrated into the roof sheathing in the form of a roll or blanket-like batt, or it can be sprayed on.

When a radiant barrier is installed, much of the heat radiated from the hot roof is reflected back toward the roof. This makes the top surface of the insulation cooler than it would have been without the barrier and reduces the amount of heat that moves through the insulation into the rooms below the ceiling. A radiant barrier has to be used with an air space. It is important that the reflective side face the air space.

Daylighting

Daylighting, or the use of natural light instead of electrical lighting, provides another way to conserve energy. Skylights have been around for years, but a newer type of product is a tubular skylight, which can be effective at reducing the need for electrical lighting during the day. The principle of the tubular skylight is the same as that of a regular skylight, but tubular skylights have smaller openings and flexible tubes that mirror and intensify the light brought into the interior of the home. Traditional skylights are harder to retrofit, require cutting a large opening in the roof, and usually need a framework around the skylight. They also do not bring in much light unless the sun is directly overhead.

A tubular skylight. Photo appears courtesy of Solatube International, Inc.

Tubular skylights have a circular opening from 10 to 21 inches in diameter and they can gather light through a clear globe when the sun is lower in the sky. The light is reflected on the interior of the flexible tubes, which can be installed through attics or even through chases or closets to a lower floor. The light is then diffused through a ceiling globe that looks somewhat like a recessed ceiling fixture.

While other types of daylighting technologies are available, tubular skylights are the most common residential application. Because daylighting does not work at night, some tubular skylights have integrated electrical lights in order to provide light both day and night.

Solar Energy

Two forms of solar energy are used in residential properties: solar heating for spaces and hot water and solar (photovoltaic) electricity.

Solar Water Heating

As the most widely used renewable energy technology, solar hot water can provide year-round hot water for residential and commercial buildings. The efficiency and reliability of solar heating systems have increased over time, reducing costs and making them attractive options.

Solar hot water is perhaps one of the most cost-effective solar technologies on the market, due to the quicker economic break-even point. Federal tax incentives available for renewable energy systems give owners an income tax credit of up to 30% of the system's cost after any state incentives, capped at $2,000 for residential systems.

Solar water heaters use the sun to heat either water or a heat-transfer fluid, such as glycol, in the collector. Heated water is then held in the storage tank ready for use, with a conventional system providing additional heating as necessary. A variety of system designs are available, depending on the climate and usage needs. The collected heat can be transferred directly to a load (such as the radiant floor heating or hot water system) or stored for later use. A solar storage tank is usually larger than a standard water heater and very well-insulated.

Today's solar water heating systems can work effectively year-round regardless of the outside temperature. In colder climates, more energy is required to heat cold incoming groundwater, so using solar energy in such conditions can dramatically lower the cost of bringing incoming water up to temperature. While a backup traditional or tankless water heater is still needed, it is used significantly less, which saves on the home's operating expenses. On average, an installed solar water heater reduces water heating bills by 50% to 80%.

The economics of solar hot water are even more attractive in new construction. Some homebuilders are beginning to list solar water heaters as an option for their homes. Others include them as a standard feature in every home. The state of Hawaii now requires solar hot water heaters for new residential construction.

Photovoltaic Cells

Another type of solar energy involves converting sunlight into electricity using photovoltaic (PV) solar panels. PV panels result in a direct conversion of solar energy into electricity. Most are mounted on roofs but some are integrated into wall panels. PV panes are currently the fastest-growing energy technology.

The basic unit of a PV panel is a photovoltaic cell, which is usually just inches wide and capable of producing one or two watts of power. Cells can be combined together to form larger units, or *modules.* These may be several feet long and several feet wide. The PV modules can then be combined into a larger group, known as an *array.*

Solar Photovoltaic Power

On-site electricity can be generated to partly or wholly provide the energy for a residence. The solar panel converts the sun's energy into direct current (DC). The DC is run through an inverter to convert it to alternating current (AC), which can then be used in the home. In some cases, more electricity is generated than is needed during certain peak periods and the excess can be sold to the local utility grid. During cloudy periods or under other circumstances, needed electricity can be repurchased.

Over 35 states have requirements for "net" electric metering. Customers are charged for the net electricity purchased from the utility company for the entire billing period. The customer benefits from the full retail rate for excess power delivered back to the utility, instead of a lower wholesale rate for PV-generated power.

The goal for many solar-powered homes is a net-zero energy system, wherein the house is self-sufficient and requires no exterior power sources.

Photovoltaic Shingles

A recent innovation in photovoltaic technology is photovoltaic shingles that can be directly applied to a roof and used instead of standard roofing shingles. This technology is also known as *building integrated photovoltaics (BIPV).* Each shingle has a wire that runs down through the roof deck and produces 17 watts in full sunlight. These shingles are flexible and are nailed on like regular shingles.

Solar Energy Incentives

In addition to the federal income tax credits mentioned earlier in this section, many incentives for the installation of solar energy are available through various state agencies and utility companies. Visit the Database of State Incentives for Renewables and Efficiency at www.dsireusa.org for a current list. Incentives may include sales tax or property tax exemptions as well as state income tax credits.

Wind Energy

Another type of renewable energy technology that is becoming more prevalent is wind power. Whether or not it is possible to install a wind turbine to harness wind energy may depend on a number of factors, such as the land available, the wind speeds available on the site, and local zoning regulations or other restrictions.

Wind turbines in a rural area of northwestern Illinois. Photo appears courtesy of Emily Ruzich.

Vertical-axis wind turbines, such as the ones shown in this photo taken in downtown Chicago, are often used in urban areas where turbulence makes it difficult to convert wind energy into power. Photo appears courtesy of Emily Ruzich.

The effectiveness of wind power is greatly dependent on the amount of wind available at a particular site. Wind speeds are divided into different classes. Typically, urban environments are in a Class 1 or Class 2 wind speed and have more inconsistency (or turbulence) than non-urban environments, making it difficult to transform wind energy into power. Because of this, some urban installations include a vertical-axis wind turbine. These turbines are designed to work more effectively in turbulent situations, although actual performance data remains inconclusive.

Much of the small-scale wind industry, especially for vertical axis machines used in urban markets, is still in an early stage of development. New standards from organizations like the Small Wind Certification Council will help instill public confidence in wind technologies.

At this time, no conclusive information about the impact of small wind turbines on residential property values in built-up areas is available. However, most wind turbine installations are placed on sites equal to or larger than one acre, likely due to the better quality of wind available.

Wind power incentives include the U.S. Department of Agriculture's Section 9006 and the Federal Residential Wind Power Tax Credit. Up-to-date state incentives can be found at www.dsireusa.org.

CHAPTER 5

Green Remodeling

Introduction

When discussing green building, the focus often tends to be on new building design and construction practices, like the LEED for Homes or NAHB Green rating systems. However, a huge market related to the renovation and remodeling of existing homes is growing and will continue to grow in the coming years. For some perspective on this issue, consider that according to the U.S. Census Bureau, www.census.gov, new construction began on approximately 600,000 single-unit residential properties in 2009, while over 76 million homes already exist in the United States.

According to the USGBC's Green Home Guide, http://greenhomeguide.com, the market for green renovation is growing even amid a downturn in the housing market at large and possibly even because of this downturn. Also, the public's awareness of green homes and their benefits is nearing a critical mass. The USGBC reports that two-thirds of homeowners are aware of green building, and 8% are extremely knowledgeable of the subject. This is an important factor in recognizing the value of green homes. Keep in mind that the commonly used definition of *market value* specifies that the buyer and seller are each acting *knowledgeably*. A difference in market value cannot be measured until the typical purchaser of a residential property is knowledgeable about the benefits of green building over conventional construction.

Nearly 40% of home remodeling in the United States is being done "green." The most commonly used green products for home remodeling projects are HVAC systems, windows, and window equipment and hardware. The following are some more facts on green remodeling compiled by the USGBC's Green Home Guide:

- The residential remodeling market has expanded by leaps and bounds over the past two decades as the median age of the U.S. existing housing stock has topped 30 years and financing options have brought costs within reach. U.S. homeowners spent $220 billion on improvement projects in 2005; this accounted for over 40% of all residential construction and nearly 2% of the U.S. economy.
- In just 10 years, nearly 30 million homes have undergone renovation and remodeling projects that exceeded 10% of the home's total value. The majority of these projects have been completed in homes valued at over $250,000. Two-thirds of these projects have taken place in homes acquired since 1990.
- Residential remodeling projects provide an opportunity to address a growing list of environmental, economic, and health concerns, such as the following:
    - Average home energy costs have reached $3,800 per year.
    - From 1980 to 1994, the number of Americans suffering from asthma increased by 75% in the general population and by 160% among children. Green remodeling can improve indoor air quality.
    - The residential sector is responsible for roughly 20% of all U.S. carbon emissions.
- In a 2005 survey, six out of 10 U.S. homeowners said they would consider integrating sustainable design practices into a future home improvement project, provided those enhancements were cost-competitive. These findings suggest that the market for green design products and services for the home may be more extensive than previously reported.

Frequently Asked Questions about Green Remodeling

The following discussion examines some frequently asked questions regarding green remodeling.[1]

What Is Green Remodeling?

Green remodeling can be defined as remodeling that incorporates energy efficiency, water and resource conservation, sustainable or recycled products, and indoor air quality considerations. The increased

1. Much of the information in this section has been compiled from the National Association of Home Builders' Web site, www.nahb.org.

availability of education for builders, growing consumer awareness, and the exploding market for environmentally friendly recycled building products has accelerated green remodeling into the mainstream.

What Are the Benefits of Green Remodeling?

Green homeowners enjoy knowing they are doing something good for the environment, their family, and the future by saving energy and precious resources. Green remodeling is good for the community, too. By using fewer materials and generating less waste, green remodeling can help lower waste management fees, achieve recycling goals, and delay the need for new power sources. Energy-efficient remodeling projects can dramatically lower energy bills.

Who Does Green Remodeling?

The NAHB offers the Certified Green Professional designation to provide homebuyers with additional assurance that the remodeler they have chosen is "green." Builders, remodelers, and other industry professionals must have at least two years of building industry experience to apply for this designation. They must also complete specific educational requirements, agree to continuing education requirements, and sign a code of ethics.

How Big Is Green Remodeling?

Green remodeling may be bigger than commonly imagined. According to a survey conducted by the NAHB, 85% of remodelers use low-energy windows, 68% use insulated exterior doors, and 65% upgrade insulation. Over 75% of remodelers use building techniques that minimize lumber impact on old-growth forests, such as alternatives to dimensional lumber, and 65% incorporate recycled or recyclable materials into their projects.

REGREEN Residential Remodeling Guidelines

The REGREEN Residential Remodeling Guidelines are different from the LEED rating systems. The REGREEN guidelines were developed in partnership by the American Society of Interior Designers (ASID) Foundation and the USGBC. Unlike LEED, the REGREEN guidelines are not a rating system and do not award points. The REGREEN guidelines are aimed at residential remodelers and interior designers. They provide best practice and environmentally responsible guidelines for homeowners, design professionals, contractors, and product suppliers.[2]

---

2. Much of the information in this section has been gathered from the *REGREEN (ASID & USGBC) Residential Remodeling Guidelines*, 2nd ed. (Washington, D.C.: ASID and USGBC, 2008). This document is available at www.regreenprogram.org. Direct link: http://www.regreenprogram.org/docs/regreen_guidelines.pdf/.

According to REGREEN, www.regreenprogram.org, the REGREEN Residential Remodeling Guidelines are the nation's first set of resources and tools for green home remodeling projects. The guidelines address the major elements of any green renovation project, including the site of the home, water efficiency, energy and atmosphere, materials and resources, and indoor environmental quality. These guidelines combine product selection, building systems integration, and proven technologies into a compilation of green strategies for the homeowner, builder, and designer. The REGREEN guidelines can be applied to a variety of home projects, such as remodeling a kitchen or bathroom, finishing a basement or attic, weatherizing a home, performing an energy retrofit, adding a major addition, redoing a back yard, or executing a gut rehab. Homeowners can either use the guidelines for their own do-it-yourself projects or visit with a professional who can implement the guidelines.

Background

The following aspects of green remodeling make it unique:

- Range of projects
  Residential remodeling covers everything from painting a room to refitting a kitchen to gutting a whole house down to the framing and then rebuilding.
- Existing conditions
  In new home construction, usually just the site needs to be considered. However, in residential remodeling existing conditions to consider can range from room configuration to hazards such as mold, lead, and asbestos.
- Custom nature of the work
  Whether in design or construction, just about every residential remodeling project is custom, with little opportunity for the sorts of economies of scale that occur in production building.
- Building the professional/client relationship
  Remodeling professionals almost always have a client, and this close relationship to homeowners requires skills and perspectives that are not generally required for new construction projects.
- Occupants
  Remodeling professionals must plan and often conduct their work based on the health, safety, and schedules of the home's occupants. Even if the work requires that the home be vacated, the timing and duration of such a period must be very carefully orchestrated.

- Sequenced or phased projects
  Many residential remodeling projects are sequenced or phased projects, such as redoing the bathroom and then the kitchen. This can make for challenging orders of operation in both design and construction, often requiring innovation and improvisation by remodeling professionals.
- Integration
  A cornerstone of all types of green building is systems integration, and residential remodeling integrates the old with the new.

These aspects of residential remodeling mean that separate resources and a separate approach are needed for green residential remodeling. Because of this, a program focused around a best practices guide rather than a rating program makes sense. This helps explain why many have struggled with developing a points-based rating system for residential remodeling and explains the evolution of the REGREEN guidelines and case studies.

Using REGREEN

The first step in using the REGREEN guidelines is picking a project type. The guidelines are based on the following 10 project types:

1. Kitchen remodel
2. Bathroom remodel
3. Bedroom remodel
4. Living and working space remodel
5. Finished basement
6. Home performance
7. Major addition
8. Gut rehab
9. Deep energy retrofit
10. Outdoor living

Each project type is then explored in terms of three major elements:

1. Integrated predesign issues
   Many of the most significant opportunities for reducing the environmental impact of a residential remodeling project lie in the decisions made at the very start of a project. The integrated predesign issues portion of the guidelines provides guidance as to what types of key questions should be asked in the beginning stages of a project.

2. Strategies
   The guidelines provide the most important green remodeling strategies that apply to each type of project listed around an illustration of such a project. These strategy lists are organized by building system or sequence in an order that represents how a remodeling professional (or informed client) would typically think about a project.
3. Project case study
   For each of the 10 project types, a representative green remodeling project is explained through a discussion of key elements of design and construction, photographs, and comments from the designer, builder, and client.

The REGREEN guidelines also include a Strategy Library, which contains nearly 200 descriptions of different types of green remodeling strategies, such as installing programmable thermostats, providing a rainwater collection system, and choosing environmentally preferable carpet and rug products. These strategy descriptions include

- A general description of the strategy, including what it entails and what it means in terms of reduced environmental impact
- Potential issues including positive synergies that can be accomplished by considering other strategies along with the one at hand, possible unintended consequences of the strategy, and issues related to cost, feasibility, etc.
- Related strategies in terms of synergies, unintended consequences, or likely partner strategies
- References and resources for additional guidance on each strategy
- Images, including photographs and architectural details, that provide further illustration and clarification

The following section provides a summary of what the REGREEN guidelines have to say about kitchen remodeling.

Kitchen Remodel

Chapter 1 of this book discussed the importance of integrating design as it is a key aspect of green building. The REGREEN guidelines address integrated design in a kitchen remodeling project as explained in the following discussion.

Integrated Predesign Issues

REGREEN presents the following questions to be addressed in a typical kitchen remodel, broken down by topic category:

- Function
  What does the client want and need?
- Existing conditions
  What functional or performance problems that exist in the kitchen space could be addressed at the design level early in the project?
- Scope
  What aspects of this project should be considered, given issues of access and timing of future work?
- Size
  Can the kitchen remodel be accomplished with the reconfiguration of existing kitchen space, does it require expansion of the kitchen into adjacent interior space, or will the kitchen remodel involve additional new space that expands the building envelope?
- Layout/space planning
  How will the kitchen space planning strike a balance between utility, aesthetics, and resource efficiency, especially energy and water use?

Strategies

The following list shows some sample strategies, organized by building system, presented for a kitchen remodel in the REGREEN guidelines. In the guidelines, a code is listed after each strategy that refers the user to a specific section and individual strategy found in the Strategy Library.

- General design and construction strategies
  - Ensure durability
  - Manage noise
  - Design with air quality in mind
  - Design for a sustainable lifestyle
  - Employ universal design
  - Design for storage
  - Provide a pantry
  - Design a practical and useable kitchen recycling system
  - Manage construction and demolition waste
  - Control the spread of pollutants
  - Install mats at exterior doors

- Building envelope
  - Upgrade or replace existing windows and doors
  - Isolate attached garages
  - Use FSC-certified wood
- Plumbing system
  - Reconfigure plumbing to distribute domestic hot water efficiently
  - Install a low-water kitchen faucet
  - Install an on-demand hot water recirculation system
  - Install a water filtration system under the sink
  - Include a plumbing access panel
- HVAC system
  - Install effective kitchen ventilation
  - Provide appropriate venting of all combustion-based heating and water heating equipment
  - Make sure ducting is clean
- Lighting and electrical systems
  - Provide daylighting
  - Provide an appropriate mix of color-correct ambient and task lighting
  - Install energy-efficient electric lighting
  - Provide shading for skylights as needed
- Appliances
  - Install an energy-efficient refrigerator
  - Choose an energy-efficient dishwasher
  - Install energy-efficient cooking appliances
  - Consider the energy toll of small appliances
  - Manage phantom loads (i.e., electricity consumed by appliances when they are switched off or in standby mode)
- Walls and ceilings
  - Install environmentally preferable interior sheathing
  - Use non-paper-faced gypsum board in moist areas
  - Limit use of wall coverings in high-moisture areas
  - Use low- or zero-VOC interior paints and finishes
  - Use appropriate sheens for paints and finishes

- Use low- or zero-VOC construction adhesives, caulking, and sealants
- Consider tile and tile trim pieces with recycled content

- Floors and flooring products
  - Consider the reuse of existing flooring and subflooring
  - Refinish wood floors using environmentally preferable processes and products
  - Choose hard-surface flooring
  - Consider flooring made from certified or reclaimed wood
  - Consider flooring made from natural or rapidly renewable materials
  - Avoid carpeting in high-moisture areas or places where spills may occur
- Furniture and fittings
  - Choose furniture and fittings that will not absorb moisture
  - Select compact furniture that incorporates storage
  - Consider reusing clean existing cabinetry or buying salvaged materials
  - Select cabinets made from greener materials
  - Evaluate the use of cabinetry and furniture made from particleboard or medium-density fiberboard
  - Install environmentally preferable countertops
  - Select materials that are easy to clean
- Use
  - Set water temperature no higher than necessary
  - Use environmentally preferable cleaning materials and strategies
  - Properly maintain equipment
  - Install carbon monoxide and smoke alarms
  - Educate homeowners on “green living”

As mentioned previously, the guidelines also provide references to specific strategies that are detailed in the guidelines’ Strategy Library. “Ensuring durability,” the first strategy listed for a kitchen remodel under the “general design and construction strategies” subheading, is discussed in the Strategy Library as follows:

> Durability applies to design, materials, and construction. It means combining these in such a way that the project responds to forces that challenge its dur-

ability–water, wind, ultraviolet radiation, pests, use and abuse, and natural disasters. It is also about designing a project with lasting aesthetics and utility. Ensuring durability involves quality assurance (of design and material selection) and quality management (construction). To ensure durability, carry out a durability evaluation, such as that called for in the LEED for Homes program, or use the building assessment form (appendix)...Designing for durability is about integrating energy efficiency with indoor air quality, energy efficiency with moisture management, and materials selection with all three. In remodeling, all of these need to be integrated with the existing home.

The guidelines then continue with a list of strategies that are related to ensuring durability as well as references to other resources on this topic.

Case Study

The guidelines also provide a case study of an exemplary kitchen remodeling project.

The clients were looking for a way to redesign their kitchen within the existing space of their concrete masonry home and were sold on the idea of building green. The tiny kitchen in this 1,200-sq.-ft. home, originally built in 1948, was poorly laid out and poorly furnished but adjoined a large mudroom (i.e., a room designed as a barrier between the outdoors and indoors for the shedding of dirty shoes and outerwear).

Reconfiguring the floor plan to subdivide the mudroom allowed the designer to expand the kitchen and add a guest bathroom without creating an addition or significantly relocating existing walls. Because the owners wanted to grow old in the building, every effort was made to ensure accessibility in the open plan. And although this project did not include a photovoltaic (PV) or graywater system, the remodel did include prewiring for a future PV system and preplumbing for graywater.

The REGREEN guidelines' case study kitchen before it was remodeled. Photo appears courtesy of REGREEN.

The next set of photos show how the kitchen remodel project turned out.

Bamboo and FSC-certified maple cabinets in the REGREEN guidelines' case study kitchen. Photos appear courtesy of REGREEN.

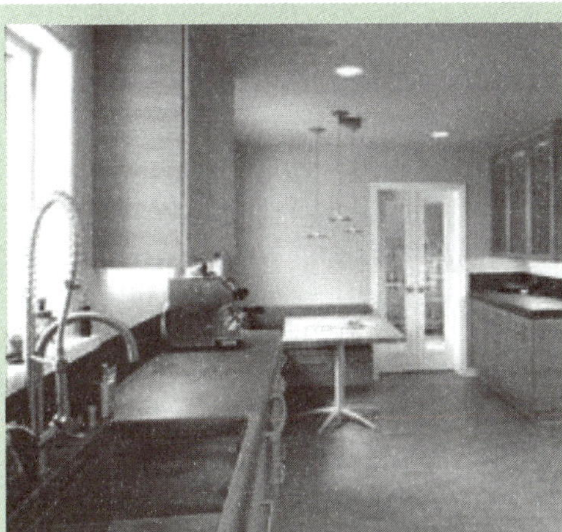

A concrete countertop with natural wax finish and a built-in eating area in the REGREEN guidelines' case study kitchen. Photos appear courtesy of REGREEN.

Concord Retrofit House

A case study of an environmentally conscious remodel of a Concord, Massachusetts home that was originally documented in *High Performing Buildings* magazine provides a good example of a thoughtful remodel, even though it did not necessarily follow the REGREEN Guidelines.[3] This particular home is an American Foursquare, originally ordered from the Sears Roebuck catalog and built in 1915. It was constructed in the Sears factory, disassembled, and shipped to the site by railroad. Then it was carefully put together on site following detailed instructions from Sears.

At the time the home was remodeled in 2007, it contained 1,000 square feet of gross living area on each floor, plus an unfinished basement and unfinished attic. Four rooms were situated on each floor of the home and because of its style, each room was situated in a corner with cross ventilation and daylighting. The home also had its original wiring, plumbing, and oil-fired boiler. The single bath and kitchen were old and in bad condition. However, the interior had beautiful plaster walls, wood trim, and maple floors. The owners wanted to retain the style and charm of the original house; they wanted to leave the exterior look and dimensions of the home intact as well as retain the original walls, floors, and trim.

The Concord Retrofit House in Concord, Massachusetts. Photo appears courtesy of Betsy Pettit, Building Science Corporation.

The remodeling project entailed a new kitchen and bath, new insulation and wiring, and new HVAC systems. One of the four second-floor bedrooms was converted into a full

3. Much of the information in this case study was gathered from the article "A Home for the Next 100 Years" by Betsy Pettit, which appeared in the Spring 2009 issue of *High Performing Buildings* magazine, published by the American Society of Heating, Refrigerating and Air-Conditioning Engineers (ASHRAE).

bath and laundry room, 600 square feet of the attic was finished into a bedroom and full bath, and 1,000 square feet of the basement was finished into a recreation room, exercise room, and half bath. New high-efficiency windows were also installed. The old aluminum siding was stripped to the wooden board sheathing.

All six sides of the building cube were wrapped with insulation and air and moisture barriers, as shown in Exhibit 5.1.

The roof received new asphalt shingles over new plywood sheathing and 2-inch rigid insulation on top of the existing roof sheathing and rafters, as shown in Exhibit 5.2.

Two new high-efficiency (92% efficient) gas boilers and air handlers for air conditioning were installed in the attic and basement in

Exhibit 5.1 Air and Moisture Barriers and Insulation of the Concord Retrofit House

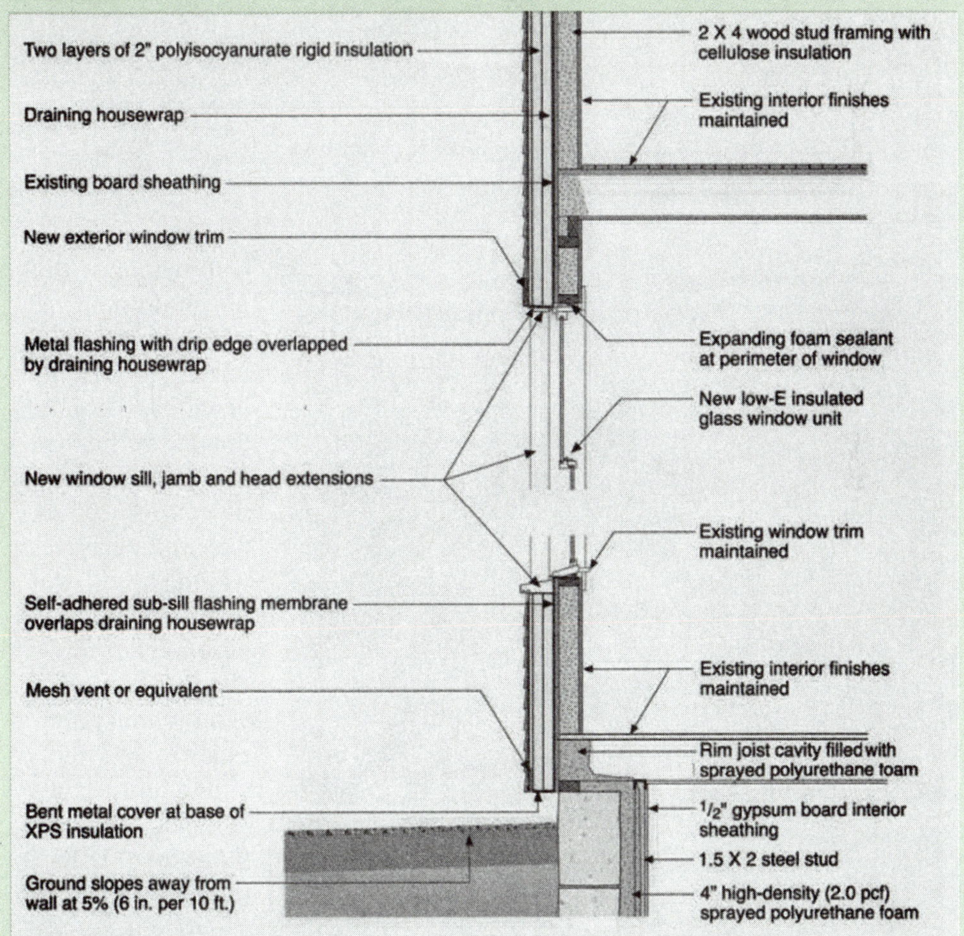

Source: Betsy Pettit, Building Science Corporation.

Exhibit 5.2 **Roofing and Insulation of the Concord Retrofit House**

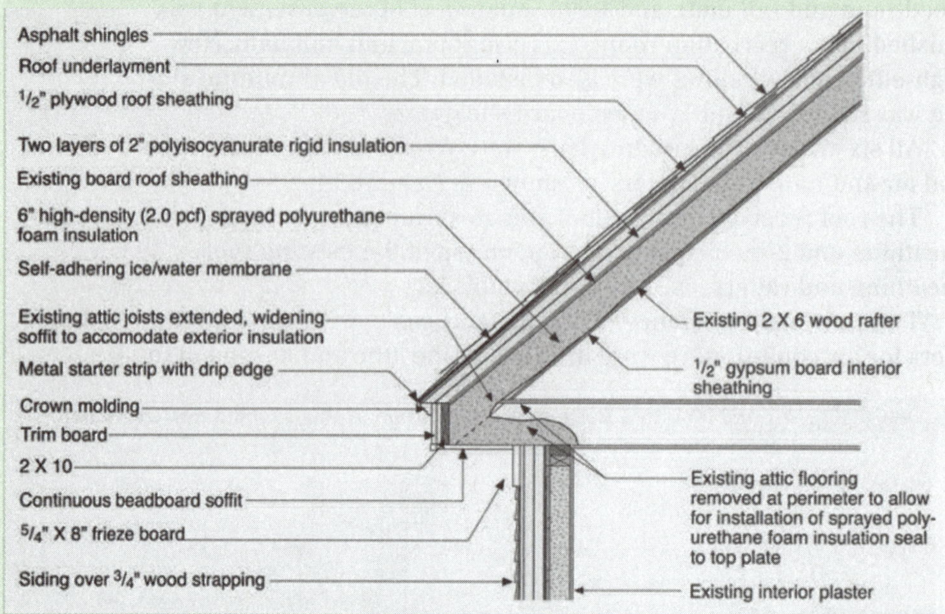

Source: Betsy Pettit, Building Science Corporation.

The Concord Retrofit House as it is being remodeled. Photo appears courtesy of Betsy Pettit, Building Science Corporation.

conjunction with the new hot water heating system; the fixture in the attic was installed to handle the newly finished attic and second floor, while the fixture in the basement would supply heat to the first floor and basement. A mechanically controlled ventilation system made up of filters with a minimum efficiency reporting value (MERV) rating of 13 was also installed to supply fresh air throughout the house. Exhibit 5.3 shows the airflow design of the remodeled home.

The basement walls received four inches of spray foam insulation and then were finished off with gypsum board over steel studs. A home energy rater ran air leakage and blower door tests on the home. Also, thermal infrared camera scans were done to detect air leaks in the building envelope. The house also received Energy Star appliances and CFL light bulbs throughout.

The bar graph in Exhibit 5.4 is illustrative of the home's savings in terms of energy consumption. The column on the left illustrates the total energy use before the renovation. The house had originally been consuming about 275 million British Thermal Units (Btu) per year. Most of that went toward heating costs (the lowest portion of the bar). The second column shows the projected energy use of a benchmark home, built to the 2007 International Code Council's En-

Exhibit 5.3 Airflow Design of the Concord Retrofit House

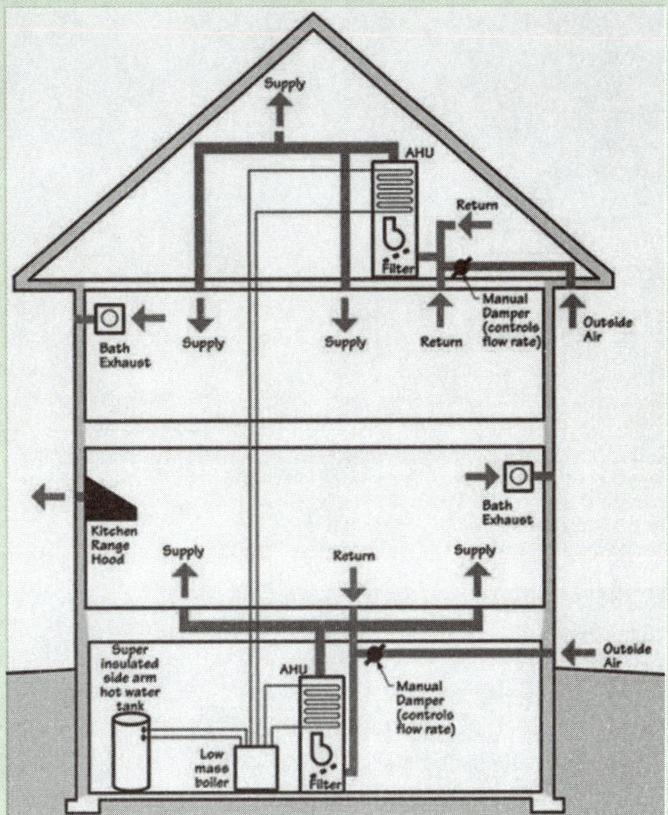

Source: Betsy Pettit, Building Science Corporation.

Exhibit 5.4 Energy Use in the Concord Retrofit House Before and After Renovation

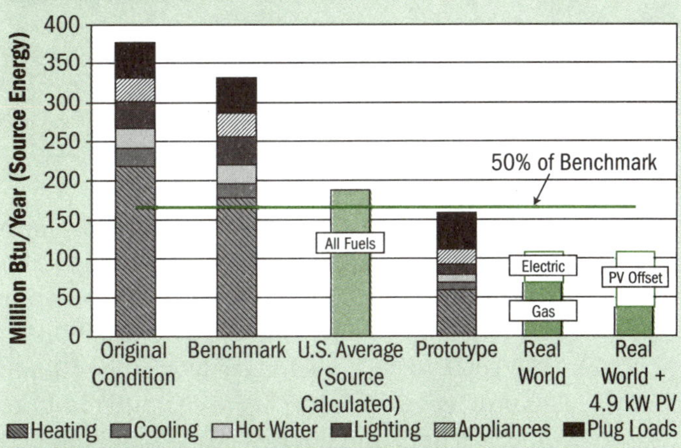

Source: Betsy Pettit, Building Science Corporation.

Mechanical system upgrades made in the basement of the Concord Retrofit House include an air handler, high-efficiency boiler, and super-insulated water tank. Photo appears courtesy of Betsy Pettit, Building Science Corporation.

The beginning stages of installing PV panes with microinverters on the shed to further offset the Concord Retrofit House's total energy use. Photo appears courtesy of Betsy Pettit, Building Science Corporation.

ergy Code. The third column shows the average energy consumption of all U.S. homes, including all fuel sources, which amounts to about 175 million Btu.

The fourth column shows the prototype energy use, which is the amount projected by computer modeling for the remodeled home after completion; this would have brought the energy use down to about 160 million Btu. The fifth column shows actual figures. The subject house actually beat the projections and for the first two years averaged only about 110 million Btu for electric and gas. The last column in Exhibit 5.4 shows the projected use of gas only. The homeowners were in the process of installing solar PV panels on the roof of a new carriage shed being built in the rear yard. After that, the total energy use would be reduced to about 40 million Btu, and the electricity would be supplied by the solar panels.

The total renovation costs for this home were approximately $300,000, or $83 per square foot, including the additional 1,600 square feet of gross living area added in the basement and attic, the new kitchen, and the two and a half baths. The cost to provide energy improvements alone came to a total of about $75,000.

CHAPTER 6

Green Appraisal Issues

Many of the green building features discussed throughout this book are relatively recent and may be new to many appraisers. It is important that the appraiser makes a conscious effort during the physical inspection of a property to look for green design features or materials and energy-efficient improvements and list and report them in a proper fashion, if they are relevant.

Due diligence requires that the appraiser adequately describe the features of the property. The market will determine whether or not an incremental value will accrue to specific green features. As appraisers, we need to be diligent in our research. Green features are a "moving target," as market consciousness and acceptance of these items will change over time.

The URAR Form

The standard Uniform Residential Appraisal Report (URAR), Fannie Mae Form 1004/Freddie Mac Form 70, only addresses green building features in two places.[1]

1. The improvements section on page 1 of the form includes a space of about one and one-half blank lines for "Additional features (special energy efficient items, etc.)" to be addressed, as shown in Exhibit 6.1. This does not provide enough space to describe a home that includes many of the features and technologies covered in this book, but these remarks can be continued in the addendum of the report. A previous entry line for insulation was deleted in

1. All information on Fannie Mae forms presented in this chapter refers to the 2005 versions of the forms, which are the most recent as of this printing.

Exhibit 6.1 **URAR Form "Additional Features" Lines**

General Description	Foundation	Exterior Description materials/condition	Interior materials/condition
Units ☐ One ☐ One with Accessory Unit	☐ Concrete Slab ☐ Crawl Space	Foundation Walls	Floors
# of Stories	☐ Full Basement ☐ Partial Basement	Exterior Walls	Walls
Type ☐ Det. ☐ Att. ☐ S-Det./End Unit	Basement Area sq. ft.	Roof Surface	Trim/Finish
☐ Existing ☐ Proposed ☐ Under Const.	Basement Finish %	Gutters & Downspouts	Bath Floor
Design (Style)	☐ Outside Entry/Exit ☐ Sump Pump	Window Type	Bath Wainscot
Year Built	Evidence of ☐ Infestation	Storm Sash/Insulated	Car Storage ☐ None
Effective Age (Yrs)	☐ Dampness ☐ Settlement	Screens	☐ Driveway # of Cars
Attic ☐ None	Heating ☐ FWA ☐ HWBB ☐ Radiant	Amenities ☐ Woodstove(s) #	Driveway Surface
☐ Drop Stair ☐ Stairs	☐ Other Fuel	☐ Fireplace(s) # ☐ Fence	☐ Garage # of Cars
☐ Floor ☐ Scuttle	Cooling ☐ Central Air Conditioning	☐ Patio/Deck ☐ Porch	☐ Carport # of Cars
☐ Finished ☐ Heated	☐ Individual ☐ Other	☐ Pool ☐ Other	☐ Att. ☐ Det. ☐ Built-in

IMPROVEMENTS

Appliances ☐ Refrigerator ☐ Range/Oven ☐ Dishwasher ☐ Disposal ☐ Microwave ☐ Washer/Dryer ☐ Other (describe)

Finished area above grade contains: Rooms Bedrooms Bath(s) Square Feet of Gross Living Area Above Grade

Additional features (special energy efficient items, etc.)

Describe the condition of the property (including needed repairs, deterioration, renovations, remodeling, etc.).

Are there any physical deficiencies or adverse conditions that affect the livability, soundness, or structural integrity of the property? ☐ Yes ☐ No If Yes, describe

Does the property generally conform to the neighborhood (functional utility, style, condition, use, construction, etc.)? ☐ Yes ☐ No If No, describe

the 2005 revision of this form, leaving even less space for appraisers to address what may be a considerable number of features.

In this part of the form, the appraiser should report what he or she knows about the insulation as well as other items that may be present, such as Energy Star appliances; energy-efficient windows, doors, and air conditioning; and insulated basement walls, pipes, and ducts. If the home is certified under one of the rating systems discussed in this book, be sure to identify that as well.

2. The second place on the URAR where energy-efficient items are addressed is in the sales comparison approach grid on page 2 of the form, as shown in Exhibit 6.2. This part of the form is where an adjustment may be made for the effect on value, if any, of all the items so carefully detailed on page 1. These items may or may not have an effect on value. The comparable sale or sales may have similar energy-efficient items so that no adjustment is warranted, or the market may not recognize the value of such energy-efficient items at the time of the appraisal.

   Fannie Mae addresses this issue in their 2009 *Selling Guide* as follows:

   > An energy-efficient property is one that uses cost-effective design, materials, equipment, and site orientation to conserve nonrenewable fuels. Special energy-saving items must be recognized in the appraisal process. The nature of these items and their contribution to value will vary throughout the country because of climatic conditions and differences in utility costs. Appraisers must compare the energy-efficient features

Exhibit 6.2 **URAR Form Sales Comparison Approach Grid**

There are comparable properties currently offered for sale in the subject neighborhood ranging in price from $ to $.
There are comparable sales in the subject neighborhood within the past twelve months ranging in sale price from $ to $.

SALES COMPARISON A

FEATURE	SUBJECT	COMPARABLE SALE # 1		COMPARABLE SALE # 2		COMPARABLE SALE # 3	
Address							
Proximity to Subject							
Sale Price	$		$		$		$
Sale Price/Gross Liv. Area	$ sq. ft.	$ sq. ft.		$ sq. ft.		$ sq. ft.	
Data Source(s)							
Verification Source(s)							
VALUE ADJUSTMENTS	DESCRIPTION	DESCRIPTION	+(-) $ Adjustment	DESCRIPTION	+(-) $ Adjustment	DESCRIPTION	+(-) $ Adjustment
Sale or Financing Concessions							
Date of Sale/Time							
Location							
Leasehold/Fee Simple							
Site							
View							
Design (Style)							
Quality of Construction							
Actual Age							
Condition							
Above Grade Room Count	Total Bdrms. Baths	Total Bdrms. Baths		Total Bdrms. Baths		Total Bdrms. Baths	
Gross Living Area	sq. ft.	sq. ft.		sq. ft.		sq. ft.	
Basement & Finished Rooms Below Grade							
Functional Utility							
Heating/Cooling							
Energy Efficient Items							
Garage/Carport							
Porch/Patio/Deck							
Net Adjustment (Total)		☐ + ☐ -	$	☐ + ☐ -	$	☐ + ☐ -	$
Adjusted Sale Price		Net Adj. %		Net Adj. %		Net Adj. %	

of the subject property to those of comparable properties in the sales comparison analysis grid to ensure that the overall contribution of these items is reflected in the market value of the subject property.[2]

Energy-Efficient Mortgages

Energy-efficient mortgages (EEMs) make it easier for borrowers to qualify for loans to purchase homes with specific energy-efficiency improvements. EEMs are available as conventional loans and through the Federal Housing Administration (FHA) and U.S. Department of Veterans Affairs (VA). They can be used to purchase new houses or to finance energy-efficient improvements in existing homes.

For a home to qualify for an EEM, a certified Home Energy Rating System (HERS) report must be prepared by an approved energy rater. The HERS report for an existing home includes

- An overall rating score for the house "as is"
- Recommended energy upgrades

2. Fannie Mae, *Selling Guide* (single-family) (April 1, 2009), 470. Available at www.efanniemae.com. Direct link: https://www.efanniemae.com/sf/guides/ssg/sg/pdf/sg0309.pdf/.

- Estimates of the annual savings and useful life of the upgrades
- The improved rating score after the upgrades are made
- The estimated total annual energy costs before and after the upgrades

A HERS rating usually costs between $200 and $400. This cost may be financed as part of the mortgage. The rating certificate is sent to the lender to evaluate the rating. If the home qualifies for energy improvements, funds are held in escrow at the closing to pay for the improvements.

Exhibit 6.3 presents a monetary comparison between a conventional mortgage and an energy-efficient mortgage. Energy-efficient mortgages allow consumers to buy more home–either through a traditional 2% stretch, which adds energy savings to income to qualify buyers for 2% more debt, or through flexible loan-to-value ratios of up to 100% of the home's value. A savings of $50 per month could translate into an additional $12,000 to $15,000 of buying power. Many standard EEMs have no upper-income restrictions, while other types of EEMs are available for borrowers who are at or below 100% of the area median income. When arranging financing, some lenders may also increase a buyer's debt ratio (the maximum percentage of gross monthly income that can be borrowed).

Federal Housing Administration

The following is a summary of FHA mortgage insurance requirements for EEMs compiled from the U.S. Department of Housing and Urban Development (HUD), www.hud.gov.

- The borrower must be eligible for a maximum FHA-backed loan, using standard underwriting procedures. The borrower must make a 3% cash investment in the property based on the sale price. Closing costs are not included in the 3% calculation but may be used to satisfy the requirement. Any upfront mortgage insurance premium can be financed as part of the mortgage.

Exhibit 6.3 Comparison of Standard and Energy-Efficient Mortgages

	Standard Home	Energy-Efficient Home
Purchaser price	$200,000	$203,000
Borrower contribution	$6,000	$6,090
Loan amount	$160,000	$162,400
Interest	5.85%	5.85%
Monthly principal, interest, taxes, and insurance	$1,673	$1,698
Average electric bill	$186	$93
Total expenses	$1,859	$1,791
Qualifying income	$49,000	$48,584
Monthly savings		$68

Based on information from the Alliance to Save Energy (ASE), http://ase.org/.

- Eligible properties are one- to four-unit existing properties and new construction.
- The cost of the energy-efficient improvements that may be eligible for financing in the mortgage is either 5% of the property's value (not to exceed $8,000), or $4,000, whichever is greater.
- To be eligible for inclusion in this mortgage, the energy-efficient improvements must be cost effective, meaning that the total cost of the improvements is less than the total present value of the energy saved over the useful life of the energy improvement. This should be calculated by a third-party home energy rater. For example, if the home energy savings would be $1,000 a year and the energy-efficient improvements would have a useful life of 12 years, the present value of $1,000 per year for 12 years, discounted at 7%, would be equal to $7,942.69.
- The cost of the energy improvements and the estimate of the energy savings must be determined by a home energy rating report, which is prepared by a home energy rating system or third-party energy consultant. The cost of the energy rating may be financed as part of the cost-effective energy package.
- The energy improvements are installed after the loan closes. The lender will place the money in an escrow account. The money will be released to the borrower after an inspection verifies that the improvements are installed and the energy savings will be achieved.
- The maximum mortgage amount for a single unit depends on its location and is adjusted annually. The cost of the eligible energy-efficient improvements is added to the mortgage amount. The final loan amount can exceed the maximum mortgage limit by the amount of the energy-efficient improvements.

U.S. Department of Veterans Affairs

The following is a summary of the VA program for EEMs from the Alliance to Save Energy, http://ase.org/.

> The VA guarantees mortgage loans for veterans with active duty service and qualified reservists. Its EEM can be used to purchase or refinance a home along with the cost of making energy-efficient improvements. To cover the cost of the improvements, the loan amount can be increased
>
> - Up to $3,000, based solely on documented costs
> - Up to $6,000, if the increase in the mortgage payment is offset by the expected reduction in utility costs
> - More than $6,000, based on a value determination by VA
>
> A VA refinancing loan may not exceed 90% of the home's appraised value plus the costs of the improvements.

Fannie Mae and Freddie Mac

Fannie Mae allows lenders to increase the ratios on the debt-to-income requirements by 2% for EEMs. Fannie Mae also allows estimated monthly energy savings to be added to income for qualification purposes and the value of the home to be adjusted to reflect the value of the energy-efficiency measures. The adjustment to the appraisal is capped at 5% of the home's value for new construction and 15% for the installed cost of retrofits.

Freddie Mac allows the lender to use the projected utility savings as a "compensating factor." Energy-efficient mortgages have been around for years but have not gained much market share. The Energy Efficiency in Housing Act of 2009 was introduced into the U.S. Senate in June of 2009. As of this writing, it has not been enacted. If this bill is passed, it would direct the Secretary of HUD to establish annual energy-efficiency participation incentives for HUD programs, budget-neutral incentives to encourage lenders to make energy-efficient and location-efficient mortgages, incentives for increasing the energy-efficiency of multiunit housing, and an energy-efficiency demonstration program for multiunit housing projects.

The bill would also require the Director of the Federal Housing Finance Agency (FHFA) to assign an additional housing credit for compliance with Fannie Mae and Freddie Mac housing goals for EEMs and require the HUD Secretary to establish a commission to develop model mortgage products and underwriting guidelines that provide market-based incentives to incorporate energy-efficiency upgrades and location efficiencies in new mortgage loan transactions. Finally, this bill would require Fannie Mae and Freddie Mac to develop loan products and flexible underwriting guidelines to facilitate a secondary market for energy-efficient and location-efficient mortgages for low- and moderate-income families and for second and junior mortgages made for purposes of energy efficiency or renewable energy.

A companion bill, the Green Act of 2009, was introduced in the U.S. House of Representatives in May of 2009. It has not passed as of this writing. It is apparent that actions are in the works, and if they are not passed in the near future, they probably will be introduced again.

Market Analysis

Market analysis is an integral part of any appraisal. Appraisers must seek adequate, market-based support for any element or component of value. If a green residential property is being appraised, the green features of the property may require added emphasis. To value the property competently, the appraiser must understand the application and implementation of sustainability principles in the development, construction, and operation of a green building and identify those benefits that are adequately supported by market evidence and may affect property value.

In the analysis of the property's local area, some questions to be answered include:

- Is the market for green homes a completely separate market?
- Do green homes compete only with other green homes or with the entire population of existing and new homes in the market area?

In many parts of the country, there may be very little sales data for new or remodeled green homes. In spite of the many advantages of green building, it is being reported by appraisers around the country that many builders are struggling to survive and are building "bare bones" homes at lower costs just to compete. Some appraisers are also reporting that builders are not interested in experimenting with new technologies or trying to sell more expensive homes in a depressed market. On the other hand, some builders who believe in sustainable concepts would rather build superior homes, even if they might cost a little more. These builders believe they actually have an advantage and can gain in market share by promoting the fact that they are building only Energy Star or LEED homes. Examples of this will be provided later in this chapter.

It is critical for appraisers to identify the mood of the market. In particular, when appraising a green home, the appraiser needs to investigate and identify supply and demand and competition in general as well as specifically for green homes. Is the subject home the only green home in the area? Are typical purchasers in that market area knowledgeable about green building? Are they willing to pay more for a green home? Or, given the choice between a green home and a non-green home, are they more willing or likely to buy a green home? Answering these questions requires the appraiser to be aware of information, trends, and economics in the market area.

Information should be gathered from market participants. Interviews with lenders, builders, buyers, sellers, real estate agents, and other appraisers may prove fruitful. Some parts of the country have excess energy and the rates are quite reasonable. It other places, energy costs are higher. Costs for electricity may range from as low as \$0.05 to \$0.20 or more per kilowatt-hour (kWh).

Also, some utility companies offer substantial rebates and incentives. High energy costs make sustainable buildings more desirable. The Database of State Incentives for Renewables and Efficiency, www.dsireusa.org, lists incentives available at the federal, state, and local levels. In addition, the USGBC, www.usgbc.org, regularly reports on new incentives that become available.

Highest and Best Use Analysis

With sustainable buildings, conventional highest and best use analysis is appropriate. Appraisers need to analyze the site as if vacant and available for its highest and best use as well as the improvements as appraised or as proposed.

As a quick reminder, the appraiser needs to measure the highest and best use using the following tests:

1. Physically possible
2. Legally permissible
3. Financially feasible
4. Maximally productive

Care should be taken in evaluating the extent to which sustainability features or attributes are found to be financially feasible or maximally productive. Two basic questions then arise.

1. Is an energy-efficient green home a higher and better use of the land as though vacant than a conventionally constructed non-green home?
2. How is the value of green features factored into the investigation of possible renovation of the existing improvements in the analysis of the highest and best use of the property as improved?

Property Description and Analysis

The physical inspection of a green residential property needs to be thorough. The appraiser should take lots of notes and photographs and note items to be investigated or researched further. The appraiser should also ask the homeowner or homeowners, if they are available, about any green features. The homeowners will most likely be happy to expound on all the details. The appraiser should also talk with the builder, if possible. A sales brochure may detail the property's green features and include estimated savings on utility costs.

If the property has a rating from an established agency or organization, a copy of the application or inspection papers should be obtained. It the property has a HERS rating, a copy should also be obtained.

The appraiser should adequately describe the extent of the inspection made and the findings in the appraisal report. The scope of work should be detailed and adequate in light of the intended use of the assignment.

The functional utility of the home should also be analyzed as the inspection is made. Marketability is the ultimate test of functional utility. The appraiser should think in terms of sustainability. As the

Exhibit 6.4 **Sample URAR Improvements Section for a Green Home Appraisal**

IMPROVEMENTS

General Description		Foundation		Exterior Description	materials/condition	Interior	materials/condition
Units ☒ One	☐ One with Accessory Unit	☐ Concrete Slab	☐ Crawl Space	Foundation Walls	IFC/good	Floors	Bamboo cpt./good
# of Stories	One	☒ Full Basement	☐ Partial Basement	Exterior Walls	SIP/good	Walls	Drywall/good
Type ☒ Det. ☐ Att.	☐ S-Det./End Unit	Basement Area	840 sq. ft.	Roof Surface	Steel/good	Trim/Finish	FSC wood/good
☒ Existing ☐ Proposed	☐ Under Const.	Basement Finish	69 %	Gutters & Downspouts	Aluminum/good	Bath Floor	Linoleum/good
Design (Style)	Ranch	☒ Outside Entry/Exit	☐ Sump Pump	Window Type	Low-E/good	Bath Wainscot	Ceramic/good
Year Built	2008	Evidence of	☐ Infestation	Storm Sash/Insulated	Triple Pane/good	Car Storage	☐ None
Effective Age (Yrs)	1	☐ Dampness	☐ Settlement	Screens	Aluminum/good	☐ Driveway	# of Cars 2
Attic	☐ None	Heating ☐ FWA ☐ HWBB	☐ Radiant	Amenities	☐ Woodstove(s) #	Driveway Surface	Perv. asphalt
☒ Drop Stair	☐ Stairs	☒ Other Ht pump	Fuel Geotherm	☐ Fireplace(s) #	☒ Fence	☒ Garage	# of Cars 2
☐ Floor	☐ Scuttle	Cooling	☒ Central Air Conditioning	☒ Patio/Deck	☐ Porch	☐ Carport	# of Cars
☐ Finished	☐ Heated	☐ Individual	☐ Other	☐ Pool	☐ Other	☒ Att. ☐ Det.	☐ Built-in

Appliances ☒ Refrigerator ☒ Range/Oven ☒ Dishwasher ☒ Disposal ☒ Microwave ☐ Washer/Dryer ☐ Other (describe) **Energy Star appliances**

Finished area **above** grade contains: 7 Rooms 3 Bedrooms 2 Bath(s) 1,680 Square Feet of Gross Living Area Above Grade

Additional features (special energy efficient items, etc.) **Energy Star home with 3rd party rating (HERS score 82). Low-E windows, low VOC paints, bamboo and linoleum floors, Energy Star fixtures, soy based spray foam insulation, low maintenance landscaping.**

Describe the condition of the property (including needed repairs, deterioration, renovations, remodeling, etc.). **The house is less than a year old and in good condition. It was constructed in an energy efficient fashion and is functionally above average. No repairs or remodeling are needed.**

Are there any physical deficiencies or adverse conditions that affect the livability, soundness, or structural integrity of the property? ☐ Yes ☒ No If Yes, describe

Does the property generally conform to the neighborhood (functional utility, style, condition, use, construction, etc.)? ☐ Yes ☒ No If No, describe **Because of its Energy Star rating and green features it has more appeal, lower maintenance costs, and lower utility costs than most houses in the neighborhood. Most of the houses in the neighborhood are 2 to 5 years old and are of conventional construction.**

world moves towards green buildings, what will happen to the 90% of existing buildings that are not green? Exhibit 6.4 shows a sample of the improvements section of the URAR form as completed for an Energy Star-rated green home.

Cost Approach

In most cases, green building features increase the energy efficiency of a home but add to its cost. The savings in energy costs may or may not offset the additional cost to construct or install the features. The cost information in Exhibit 6.5 represents a sample prepared by the McStain Neighborhoods builders in Denver, Colorado.

It would be easy to calculate the payback periods of each of the optional extras listed in Exhibit 6.5. For example, the first item (advanced framing) saves $36 per year but costs $545 to install. This indicates a payback of 545/36, or 15.1 years. This is a simplistic exercise that ignores the time value of money, but it provides a quick and easy method of comparison for consumers who would not necessarily understand discounting. In comparison, adding Low-E windows costs $210 but saves $55 per year; this means the payback period (without discounting) would only be 3.8 years, making this a sure winner.

In the final cost comparison of an energy-efficient home versus a home built to code shown in Exhibit 6.5, the additional $6,204 spent on the energy-efficient features is recouped in reduced utility payments and actually saves the homebuyer $9.51 per month after the mortgage payments and utility charges are figured in.

Estimating Costs

Residential appraisers working with existing properties may sometimes not use the cost approach. However, this approach is very appropriate for green buildings because it brings out some of the questions and features covered earlier in this book. If the cost approach is applied to value a residence that has some green features or is a full-fledged Energy Star-certified or LEED-rated home, the appraiser should make sure the home's green features are accurately accounted for in the reproduction or replacement cost estimate.

In the cost approach to value, the first question to be answered is *reproduction or replacement cost?* A reproduction cost estimate may prove to be more relevant in the case of green homes. The *Dictionary of Real Estate Appraisal*, fifth edition, defines *reproduction cost* as "the estimated cost to construct, at current prices as of the effective date of the appraisal, an exact duplicate or replica of the building being appraised, using the same materials, construction standards, design, layout, and quality of workmanship and embodying all the deficiencies, superadequacies, and obsolescence of the subject building." Since green buildings are different from conventional construction, it makes sense to use the cost of an exact replica of the green building being appraised because green buildings incorporate specific materials, construction standards, and design principles.

Trying to find replacement cost means costing out a building with equivalent utility, which may require exercising judgment and making tradeoffs. *The Dictionary of Real Estate Appraisal* defines *replacement cost* as "the estimated cost to construct, at current prices as of the effective appraisal date, a substitute for the building being appraised, using modern materials and current standards, design, and layout." A green building today would be one that uses modern materials and current standards, design, and layout. As a result,

Exhibit 6.5 Cost Information

McStain Neighborhoods

Energy Efficiency
Row Home 1733 sq. ft.

Features	~Annual Savings	~Cost premium
Advanced framing 2"x6"	$36	$545
Windows w/ low emissivity argon-fill	$55	$210
92.1% direct vent furnace	$88	$900
Water heater – sealed combustion	$22	$400
(converting to tankless water heaters-additional 45% savings)		
Advanced insulation system	$89	$975
Infiltration/advanced air sealing - (2.5 sq.in. /100 sq.ft.)	$81	$410
Sealed conditioned Crawl space	$19	$110
Engineered duct distribution system	$60	$920
•All ducted system, inside conditioned space		
•Set back digital thermostat		
Fireplace w/ Electronic ignition	$72	$0
Downsize furnace/AC	$43	-$750
Mechanical ventilation	-$10	$300
3rd Party verification and energy commissioning	$0	$580
Total	**$555**	**$4600**

McSTAIN

McStain Neighborhoods

Indoor Air Quality, Natural Resource Conservation, Durability
Row Homes 1733 sq. ft.

Features	~Cost Premium
Exterior drainage plane	$166
Finger joint studs	$0
Engineered lumber products	$136
Cementitious siding material	$0
Recycled content decking	$10
Low VOC paint and finishes	$332
Recycled PET carpet	$175
Ductwork cleaning	$300
Sealed combustion appliances incl. fireplace	$200
Blown cellulose insulation	$0
High performance bath fans	$225
Sealed sump pit cover	$60
Total:	**$1604**

McSTAIN

$236,204 Energy Efficient Home

- Length of Loan in Years 30
- Interest Rate 6%
- Loan Amount 236,204
- Annual Property Tax 1200
- Annual Insurance 400
- Monthly Principal + Interest 1416.16
- Monthly Tax 100
- Monthly Insurance 33.33
- Total Payment 1,549.49
- Monthly Utility Costs 78
- Monthly total with utilities $1,627.49

$230,000 home built to code (IECC 2003)

- Length of Loan in Years 30
- Interest Rate 6%
- Loan Amount 230,000
- Annual Property Tax 1200
- Annual Insurance 400
- Monthly Principal + Interest 1378.96
- Monthly Tax 100
- Monthly Insurance 33.33
- Total Payment 1512.29
- Monthly utility costs125.00
- Monthly total with utilities $1637

Difference of $+9.51

McSTAIN

Source: McStain Neighborhoods, www.mcstain.com.

replacement cost should essentially be the same as reproduction cost. However, most agree that because reproduction cost is preferable and gets directly to the point, it is more relevant in valuing a green building.

A reproduction cost estimate should be derived from local builders. The Marshall & Swift *Residential Cost Handbook* does not specifically address green building features. However, Marshall & Swift published a supplement, *Green Building Costs*, in 2009. *Green Building Costs*, which is available for purchase at www.marshallswift.com, contains cost information for residential and commercial green properties, including new construction and renovations. Of course, use of this manual results in replacement cost.

The following discussion presents some examples of how to calculate green building costs based on Marshall & Swift cost information. Exhibit 6.6 shows an illustration of how to fill in green building costs on the Marshall & Swift Form 1007. Exhibit 6.7. shows a section of Marshall & Swift costs for permeable paving and HVAC.

Limited information is available on the cost new of green buildings, whether for identical or highly similar buildings (reproduction cost) or generally similar buildings (replacement cost). Green building products and construction techniques are still new and costs are still changing and evolving. The best sources of costs for sustainable building features are most likely local builders and contractors. As manufacturers develop and sell more sustainable building products, the costs should continue to decrease. As contractors and subcontractors become more familiar with installation techniques, they will be able to perform them more efficiently and economically, thereby reducing installation costs.

When it comes to green homes, generalization is very difficult because there are so many differences across the country in terms of energy needs, materials, products, installation techniques, and local code requirements; and the amount of data available varies. Just because

Exhibit 6.6 Green Building Costs Recorded on Marshall & Swift Form 1007

Component	Quantity	Unit Cost	Extended Cost	Depreciation Age/Life	%	Total
Entry, Prehung, Solid, Oak, 3'0" x 6'8", Door	*1*	*$754*	*$754*			
Move to Line 25: Additional Components			*$754*			
Drip irrigation, micro sprayer kit,						
small lawn	*1*	*$141*	*$141*			
Move to Line 31: Yard Improvements			*$141*			
Wind turbine generator, off-grid, 33' guyed						
Pole, 9' rotor blade	*1*	*$18,938*	*$18,938*			
Move to Line 32: Miscellaneous			*$18,938*			

two homes are built green does not mean that they are built the same way. Some green homes may have solar panels and full underground rainwater collection systems, while other green homes may have features such as low-flow faucets, high-performance windows, and Energy Star appliances. However, it has generally been reported that the cost to build a green home usually only adds 1% to 5% above the cost of conventional construction. Exhibit 6.8 presents a comparison of the ownership costs of a LEED-rated home versus a home built to code.

Exhibit 6.7 Marshall & Swift Cost Information

PERMEABLE / POROUS PAVING

	UOM	COMMERCIAL	RESIDENTIAL
Paving, Reclaimed Brick, With 2" sand bed,			
4"x 8"x 2-1/4"	SF	$11.95	$10.55
Herringbone pattern	SF	14.90	13.00
Paving, Reclaimed, Granite, With 2" sand bed, Random,			
4"x 6" to 6"x 10"	SF	17.75	16.35
Herringbone pattern	SF	21.00	18.90
Permeable pavers, interlocking,			
2"gravel base and fill, precast concrete	SF	11.95	10.75
L-shaped, precast concrete	SF	10.60	9.65
Turf block, 8 open cells, precast concrete	SF	8.50	7.65

HVAC

This area focuses on the efficient use of energy for habitant comfort as it pertains to climate control of a building. Typically items covered may include Minimum Energy Performance, On-site Renewable Energy and Fundamental Refrigerant Management.

	UOM	COMMERCIAL	RESIDENTIAL
High efficiency gas furnace, Forced air,			
With single stage burner, 92% AFUE, 45 MBH	EA	----	$ 1,600.00
With 2 stage burner, 95% AFUE,70 MBH	EA	----	1,700.00
Variable speed blower, 95% AFUE, 115 MBH	EA	----	2,800.00
Heat pump, Geothermal, Forced air, Heat and cooling, (equipment only, add ground loop below)			
2.5 tons	EA	----	4,700.00
3 tons	EA	----	4,800.00
4 tons	EA	$ 5,350.00	5,200.00
5 tons	EA	5,725.00	5,525.00
Heat pump, Geothermal, Hydronic, Heat and cooling, (equipment only, add ground loop below)			
2.5 tons	EA	----	5,800.00
3 tons	EA	----	5,950.00
4 tons	EA	7,175.00	6,975.00
5 tons	EA	8,175.00	7,900.00
6 tons	EA	9,950.00	9,475.00

Source: Marshall & Swift's *Green Building Costs*. Reprinted with permission of Marshall & Swift/Boeckh, LLC, and its licensors, copyright 2009. May not be reprinted, copied, or automated without permission.

Exhibit 6.8 Costs of an Energy-Efficient LEED Home vs. a Conventional Home

Comparison Criteria	Code Home	LEED-Rated Home	Price Difference	
			$ per month	$ per day
Sticker price	$300,000.00	$308,500.00		
Mortgage payment	$1,890.00	$1,945.00	+$55.00	+$1.80
Energy bill	$150.00	$105.00	-$45.00	-$1.50
Water bill	$30.00	$20.00	-$10.00	-$0.30
Net cost of ownership	$2,070.00	$2,070.00	$0.00	$0.00

Based on information from the USGBC, www.usgbc.org.

Even in the case of commercial buildings, which are more complex, the increased construction costs of green building are small. According to a 2006 presentation by the Green Building Finance Consortium, the lowest level of LEED certification is associated with a 0.8% higher initial cost, LEED "silver" buildings cost 3.5% more initially, and LEED "gold" buildings cost 4.5% more initially.[3]

3. Beth Anderson, "LEED Certification Program Leads to Potential Profits," *NuWire Investor* (December 3, 2007), www.nuwireinvestor.com. Direct link: http://www.nuwireinvestor.com/articles/leed-program-leads-to-potential-profits-51367.aspx/.

One builder who has built over 50 homes to Colorado Built Green standards has reported that most green homes cost no more to build than conventional homes because the green features simply take the place of extra features, such as high ceiling entryways or whirlpool tubs. As a result, the new green homes are price competitive, healthier to live in, and can realize energy costs that are reduced by 20% or more.

Depreciation

When performing a cost approach for a sustainable house, depreciation may have to be reconsidered. The appraiser may have to exercise his or her best judgment if dealing with an existing green building and find out as much as possible about when and how the building was constructed.

The appraiser will have to make an analysis and judge the building's effective age. Then, most likely some type of age-life method (either whole property or by component) will be used to ascertain the amount of accrued physical depreciation that is present on the effective date of the appraisal. If effective age divided by total life is used, the appraiser should keep in mind that green buildings may well have lower effective lives than conventional buildings. Part of the sustainability principles include using materials that may have longer lives and require less maintenance. Current depreciation tables do not yet reflect green buildings. The market extraction of physical depreciation is problematic at this point because there are too few data points.

Functional obsolescence is an important area to consider when appraising a green home. *The Appraisal of Real Estate*, 13th edition, defines *functional obsolescence* as follows: "Functional obsolescence is caused by a flaw in the structure, materials, or design of the improvement when compared to the highest and best use and most cost-effective functional design requirements at the time of appraisal. A building that was functionally adequate at the time of construction can become inadequate or less appealing as design standards, mechanical systems, and construction materials change over time." This definition is succinct and gets right to the kernel of what has been discussed in comparing green buildings to conventional construction. Green building design standards, mechanical systems, and construction materials are changing.

As the percentage of new construction and renovations grows over the coming years, non-green buildings will eventually become functionally obsolete to some extent. It may happen gradually or rapidly, depending on the market. Green building is stratified in different market areas now and the change will depend on many disparate economic market factors, which will undoubtedly vary from region to region. To keep up, appraisers will need to be vigilant in their research.

The measurement of any functional obsolescence should be undertaken in the traditional ways. Functional obsolescence may be curable or incurable depending on whether the cost to cure will result in a value increment that is at least equal to the cost to cure. Measurements of functional obsolescence may be obtained through sales comparison analysis or through a capitalization of rent loss.

Functional obsolescence can be caused by a deficiency or a superadequacy as measured against, or compared to, market tastes and expectations. The possible superadequacy of building designs, materials, and systems should be considered. Keep in mind that superadequacies are judged according to market norms or standards. If the norm in a market area is the conventional building, then it is possible that some aspects of a new green building may be considered superadequacies.

As buildings age and market tastes and standards change, functional obsolescence is more likely to arise. However, some buildings can be constructed with functional obsolescence built in; they may be built with inadequate materials or with a poor design or layout. The real question to ask is, *when should non-green obsolescence be confronted?* The answer is, *when the marketplace begins to acknowledge it.*

Land Value

Land value should be estimated conventionally. Depending on the situation, the appraiser might employ a sales comparison technique or any of the other accepted techniques, such as allocation or extraction. In addition, site improvement costs may be atypical as different site strategies are employed. For example, less money may have been spent on paving and formal landscaping, while more money may have been spent on grading and drainage improvements.

Keep in mind that Fannie Mae and Freddie Mac forms require more information on the cost approach than they used to. Appraisers are now asked to provide adequate information for the lender or client to replicate the cost figures and calculations shown and to supply the source of the cost data provided.

Exhibit 6.9 shows an example of how a completed cost approach section on the URAR form might look for an appraisal of a green residence.

Sales Comparison Approach

The only difference that appraisers will most likely consider in the sales comparison approach for a green residential building is greater detail on the line for energy-efficient items and possibly the line for functional utility in the sales grid. The appraiser may also recognize a higher quality level. As usual, adjustments should only be made for

Exhibit 6.9 Sample URAR Cost Approach Section for a Green Home Appraisal

COST APPROACH TO VALUE (not required by Fannie Mae)

Provide adequate information for the lender/client to replicate the below cost figures and calculations.

Support for the opinion of site value (summary of comparable land sales or other methods for estimating site value) Land Sale 1: 214 Elm Street, .75 acre, 120 ft. frontage, water & sewer, sold 9/23/09 for $32,000. Land sale 2: 456 Maple Lane, 1.1 acre, 140 ft. frontage, water & sewer, sold 5/06/09 for $37,000 Land sale 3: 790 Pine Street, 1.2 acre, 150 ft. frontage, no utlities, sold 11/15/09 for @27,500.

COST APPROACH	
ESTIMATED ☐ REPRODUCTION OR ☒ REPLACEMENT COST NEW	OPINION OF SITE VALUE .... = $ 35,000
Source of cost data Marshall & Swift Residential Cost Handbook	Dwelling 1,680 Sq. Ft. @ $ 97.45 .... =$ 163,716
Quality rating from cost service Good Effective date of cost data Sep 09	Fin. Bsmnt. 550 Sq. Ft. @ $ 44.76 .... =$ 24,618
Comments on Cost Approach (gross living area calculations, depreciation, etc.)	PV panels, geothermal heat pump, gas FP 32,560
Dwelling cost figures are from M & S pages Good-15, Good-23, & Good-	Garage/Carport 480 Sq. Ft. @ $ 36.35 .... =$ 17,448
24. The cost of the PV panels and Geothermal heat pump are from the	Total Estimate of Cost-New .... = $ 238,342
Marshall & Swift Green Building Costs manual, dated December 2009,	Less Physical | Functional | External
pages 17 and 19. The house, when completed, will be brand new with no	Depreciation =$( )
Physical, Functional, or External depreciation. The site improvements will	Depreciated Cost of Improvements .... =$ 238,342
include seeded lawn, professional landscaping, and stormwater retention	"As-is" Value of Site Improvements .... =$ 18,000
pond.	
Estimated Remaining Economic Life (HUD and VA only) Years	Indicated Value By Cost Approach .... =$ 291,342

differences between the comparable sales and the subject that are significant and measurable.

Arguably, energy-efficient homes demonstrate shorter marketing times. This is a value consideration and may be worthy of note, particularly in slower markets. The measure of the differences will be market driven, and the amount of the adjustment will be based on contributory value *rather than cost*. There is no magic formula to apply. The appraiser will most likely have to rely on paired data analysis. He or she can certainly interview builders, real estate agents, buyers, and sellers to get their reactions to various sustainability aspects and make adjustments based on the capitalized value of any rent differences, if applicable. Another possibility would be to make adjustments based on the monthly energy savings multiplied by the gross rent multiplier (GRM).

Because of the newness of green building in many areas, sales activity and market evidence of value trends may be limited. In some cases, the property being appraised may be the first or one of the few sustainable homes in the area. In cases like these, the appraiser may have to use comparable sales from a wider area and may end up using a mix of conventional buildings and green buildings as the market comparables.

In other areas–such as the Denver metropolitan area, which has a 25% market share of Built Green houses–it is relatively easy to make comparisons between similar new houses that are of standard construction and those that have been built to a green building standard. The appraiser will have to undertake more research to ascertain the existence or extent of any sustainable features in the comparable sales.

Most multiple listing services (MLS) do not consistently report sustainable or energy-efficient features. If they do, the features may be described in general terms. The appraiser will have to do research and may have to interview the real estate agent to find out exactly what energy-efficient components are present in a comparable sale property. It is a good idea to contact local USGBC and NAHB chapters and other members of the green community as well as architects, real estate agents, and local developers who are producing LEED-certified buildings for information.

Of course, if a house has been designated as an Energy Star home or has a LEED for Homes rating, there will be objective standards by which to judge it. Some strides are being taken in this area. The Oregon Regional MLS has added a field for green housing, and appraisers will be able to search for new homes that have met national standards under the leading green building programs. Other MLS services are considering adding green or sustainable categorization as well.

The Green Multiple Listing Service Tool Kit, released in 2010, provides guidance on implementing green initiatives in local multiple listing services. The tool kit provides a snapshot of the green home industry, explains why green fields should be added to MLS systems, makes recommendations for implementing green MLS initiatives, and provides examples of green data entry forms. The tool kit was created by the Council of Multiple Listing Services, the Multi-Regional Multiple Listing Service, the National Association of REALTORS®, the USGBC, the Appraisal Institute, and other organizations. It is available online at www.greenthemls.org.

Exhibit 6.10 presents an example of a sales comparison grid on the URAR form that has been filled in with sample figures for a green home. In this case, differences were recognized and adjustments made for both functional utility and energy-efficient items. The support for these adjustments should be detailed in the comments section or the addendum of the appraisal report. Perhaps they can be supported by a paired data analysis or another type of study or analysis.[4] At the end of this chapter, some evidence of the increased value of green homes in the Pacific Northwest region will be presented.

Income Capitalization Approach

The benefits of a green building are probably most directly measurable through the income capitalization approach. As compared to a conventional building, a sustainable building may have

- Higher rents
- Lower vacancies
- Lower operating expenses
- Less risk

All of these factors should result in a higher net income and value. The impact is more direct and easier to measure by the income capitalization approach than the other approaches. Sustainable attributes may theoretically influence different components of the rate of return as well as the change in income or value. However, given the scarcity of data, it may be difficult to prove this point. The appraiser may place greater reliance on the income capitalization approach when valuing residential properties, particularly in two- to four-unit properties and in non-owner-occupied, single-unit residential properties being purchased or used for rental or investment.

The URAR form and Fannie Mae's Small Residential Income Property Appraisal Report (Form 1025) still use the GRM approach. The income capitalization approach is not required for single-unit

4. See Mark R. Rattermann, *Valuation by Comparison* (Chicago: Appraisal Institute, 2007) for examples of supportable adjustments for energy efficiency and quality of construction.

Exhibit 6.10 Sample URAR Sales Comparison Section for a Green Home Appraisal

Proximity to Subject		1 block East		Same street		2 blocks West	
Sale Price	$		$ 295,000		$ 285,000		$ 287,000
Sale Price/Gross Liv. Area	$ sq. ft.	$ 175.60 sq. ft.		$ 178.13 sq. ft.		$ 164.94 sq. ft.	
Data Source(s)	Inspection	MLS/Assessor		MLS/Assessor		MLS/Assessor	
Verification Source(s)	Buyer	Selling agent		Selling agent		Selling agent	
VALUE ADJUSTMENTS	DESCRIPTION	DESCRIPTION	+(-) $ Adjustment	DESCRIPTION	+(-) $ Adjustment	DESCRIPTION	+(-) $ Adjustment
Sale or Financing Concessions	N/A	Conventional None		Conventional None		Conventional None	
Date of Sale/Time		1 month ago		2 weeks ago		1 month ago	
Location	Suburban/Gd	Suburban/Gd		Suburban/Gd		Suburban/Gd	
Leasehold/Fee Simple	Fee simple	Fee simple		Fee simple		Fee simple	
Site	.5 acres	.5 acres		.5 acres		.5 acres	
View	Residential/Av	Residential/Av		Residential/Av		Residential/Av	
Design (Style)	Ranch	Ranch		Ranch		Ranch	
Quality of Construction	Good	Good		Good		Good	
Actual Age	1	1		1		1	
Condition	Good	Good		Good		Good	
Above Grade Room Count	Total 7 / Bdrms. 3 / Baths 2	Total 7 / Bdrms. 3 / Baths 2		Total 7 / Bdrms. 3 / Baths 2		Total 7 / Bdrms. 3 / Baths 2	
Gross Living Area	1,680 sq. ft.	1,680 sq. ft.		1,600 sq. ft.	+5,600	1,740 sq. ft.	-4,200
Basement & Finished Rooms Below Grade	Full - fin 550 SF	Full - fin 600 SF		Full - unf	+6,000	Full - fin 500 SF	
Functional Utility	Good-Green	Good-Green		Good-Conv	+5,000	Good-Conv	+5,000
Heating/Cooling	Heat pump	Heat pump		Heat pump		HA/CAC	
Energy Efficient Items	82 HERS score	85 HERS score		100 HERS/Av	+5,700	100HERS/Av	+5,780
Garage/Carport	2 car att	2 car att		2 car att		2 car att	
Porch/Patio/Deck	Deck	Deck		Deck		Deck	
Net Adjustment (Total)		☐ + ☐ -	$	☒ + ☐ -	$ 22,300	☒ + ☐ -	$ 6,580
Adjusted Sale Price of Comparables		Net Adj. % Gross Adj. %	$ 295,000	Net Adj. % Gross Adj. %	$ 307,300	Net Adj. 2.3 % Gross Adj. 5.2 %	$ 293,580

properties on the URAR but is required on Form 1025. The Appraisal Institute's Summary Appraisal Report–Residential (see Exhibit 6.11) has more room for a market rent analysis and comments to explain the development of the GRM analysis.

In developing the income capitalization approach, the appraiser must first estimate the gross monthly rent for each unit in the subject property. All the calculations do not have to be shown on the URAR, but a section of comparable rental data must be completed on Form 1025. Energy savings from a green building may impact the amount of rent obtainable. The appraiser should pay attention to who pays the utility costs in the rental units and whether the tenant or the landlord will therefore gain the benefit from the energy cost savings, as that is one of the direct benefits of a green building.

When calculating the appropriate GRM, the appraiser should try to use sales of sustainable buildings that were rented at the time of sale. If any of the sale properties used are green buildings, this should be taken into account when reconciling the GRM from the data and explained accordingly.

Any value conclusions developed in the income capitalization approach relative to a green building (such as a capitalized rent gain or loss) would be an appropriate basis for adjustments made in the sales comparison approach. Another measurement technique might be to multiply the GRM by the monthly utility savings.

Exhibit 6.11 GRM Section of the AI Reports® Summary Appraisal Report—Residential

Rent comparable analysis and reconciliation of market rent of subject property:

Opinion of Market Rent $

Gross Rent Multiplier Analysis

ADDRESS	DATE	SALE PRICE	GROSS RENT	GRM	COMMENTS

Comment and reconciliation of the gross rent multiplier (GRM):

Opinion of Market Rent: $ ________ × ________ GRM = $

Indication of Value by Income Approach $

Reconciliation

Most residential appraisers use the three traditional approaches to value and carry the same three tools in their bag for each assignment. For traditional residential properties, the sales comparison tool is usually used the most. When appraising a residence with sustainable characteristics, the other two tools–the cost approach and the income capitalization approach–may have to be used more.

Sales data for green residences may be scarce in some market areas. As time moves along and the green building industry matures, more data will become available. However, this data may still be spotty and unevenly distributed in some areas. Verification of green building features may be difficult and the quantification of their impact on value may be challenging, especially if the improvements have only been in place for a short time.

Appraisers may use the cost approach more effectively in some markets. While cost and value are not the same, a properly developed cost approach can be a reliable value indicator. Keep in mind that depreciation and site improvement costs may have to be treated differently. Cost data for green building features should become more readily available and reliable in the coming years.

The income capitalization approach may be applicable for certain property types and some of its findings may be used as a measure of depreciation in the cost approach or as an adjustment in the sales comparison approach.

Increased appeal, lower vacancies, and shortened marketing times may be discernible value factors in all three approaches. Market participants are more conscious of energy efficiency and resource depletion than ever before. Remember that the role of the appraiser is to be a translator. With a sustainable property, appraisers must translate the sustainable features of the property, the benefits that accrue from those features, and the market acceptance, which all lead to the market value opinion.

Do Green Homes Sell for More?

Do green homes sell for more money? According to a 2008 article in *Appraiser News Online*,

> New analysis shows "green" homes may be a bright spot in today's real estate market. Environmentally certified homes sold for 4.8% more and stayed on the market for 24% less time than comparable homes sold last year, according to GreenWorks Realty. The firm's research focused on the Seattle market.
>
> In the first year since it began tracking environmentally certified homes, 19.8% of new homes in Seattle sold on the Northwest MLS were environmentally certified. These homes averaged 1,477 square feet, just slightly smaller

> than the 1,492-sq.-ft. average for all new homes sold. On a square-foot basis, this means green homes sold for a 5.9% premium. Green homes certified by a third party sold for a 10.5% premium on a square-foot basis.[5]

It is certainly logical that green homes should sell for more than conventionally constructed homes. As the buying public becomes more and more aware of the advantages of green homes, one would expect this to be the case. However, this can only be judged on market evidence. For appraisers in Seattle, Portland, Denver, or some of the other hot spots for green building, real-world evidence already exists in the marketplace.

Certified Home Performance Study

What is probably the most comprehensive study on green building was released by the Earth Advantage Institute in May 2009. The study, *Certified Home Performance: Assessing the Market Impacts of Third-Party Certification on Residential Properties*, analyzes the market performance of certified sustainable residential properties in Portland, Oregon, and Seattle, Washington.[6]

In this study, a sample of 92 certified homes and 340 comparable homes in the Portland metropolitan area was compiled. The certified homes were built between 2000 and 2008, with the majority sold in 2006 and 2007. Most certified homes were matched with three or four comparables. Certified homes were geographically distributed throughout the metropolitan area. The study found that, in the Portland area, certified homes sold 18 days faster than noncertified homes and for 3%-5% more than noncertified homes. In a statistical analysis with a 95% level of confidence, the overall price difference was found to be 4.2%.

In Seattle, a sample of 68 certified homes and 207 comparable residences was compiled. Like the Portland sample, most certified homes were matched with three or four comparable homes. The Seattle analysis also documented superior market performance in terms of the sale price achieved. The Seattle study found that the expected percentage change in sale price was found to be 9.6% more for the third-party certified sustainable homes.

The Earth Advantage Institute, the Master Builders Association of Pierce County, and the Olympia Master Builders conducted sur-

---

5. Ben Kaufman, "Green Buildings Selling for More," *Appraiser News Online* (April 30, 2008).
6. Ann Griffin, Earth Advantage Institute, with Ben Kaufman, GreenWorks Realty, and Sterling Hamilton, Hamilton Investments, LLC, *Certified Home Performance: Assessing the Market Impacts of Third-Party Certification on Residential Properties* (May 29, 2009). Available online through the Master Builders Association of Pierce County, www.builtgreenpierce.com. Direct link: http://www.builtgreenpierce.com/media/pdf/GBVI%20Residential%20Report%20Final.pdf/.

veys of residents living in homes certified by either Earth Advantage or Built Green. The survey results indicated that residents value the sustainable attributes of their homes, particularly energy efficiency and improved indoor air quality. Of those surveyed, 90% reported that they would choose a certified home over a noncertified home for their next residence if all other factors were equal. The residents also collectively agreed that they would pay more in order to continue to live in a sustainable home. A majority (80%) of the survey respondents living in third-party certified homes reported that they would pay up to 5% more to move into a home that had been certified as sustainable over one that had not. Exhibit 6.12 shows the survey results regarding sustainable home features that respondents indicated they would be most likely to invest in.

The study also made several interesting points based on interviews with builders in the Portland/Seattle area:

- **Homebuilders believe that third-party verification adds value.** Almost all of the builders who contributed to this study (98%) stated that third-party sustainable certification adds to the value of the product. These builders equate certification efforts with a high-quality end product, superior construction, increased energy efficiency, and positive health impacts for home residents. However, these builders were also concerned that current residential appraisal practices did not sufficiently recognize the positive benefits of such a certification. Additional discussion followed regarding how market value is determined. Several builders commented that the increased value of their homes is not adequately rewarded by the market. One builder stated, "Yes, there is added value to a home [in achieving certification], but we don't just adjust the price. So it can be difficult to measure the value exactly. We are selling at cost right now in order to be competitive." Most residential appraisers may not know how to assign a dollar value to specific sustainable

Exhibit 6.12 Survey Responses

Please check/describe the particular sustainable feature or features in which you would be most likely to invest.	
Energy-efficient hot water heater/tankless water heater	89%
Energy-efficient furnace	87%
Indoor air quality	69%
Construction practices that use reclaimed/recycled materials and recycling	49%
On-site renewable energy source	42%
Graywater capture and reuse	27%
Other features	10%

Source: Based on information from *Certified Home Performance: Assessing the Market Impacts of Third-Party Certification on Residential Properties*, Earth Advantage Institute with GreenWorks Realty and Hamilton Investments, LLC.

features in a home. Additionally, standard residential appraisal documents do not include an area where this information may be recorded.

- **Home values should incorporate performance measures.** Residential performance measures should be incorporated into standard home valuation. For example, long-term reductions in home utility and repair costs should be considered when a newly built or remodeled home with sustainable and energy-efficiency features is appraised.
- **More dynamic appraisal models are needed.** Dialogue among sustainable building advocates, homebuilder associations, residential appraisers, realtors, and financial institutions regarding more accurate and dynamic residential appraisal should continue. Such a dialogue is needed to develop the mechanisms for recording sustainable improvements in a home and monitoring the ongoing performances of these improvements.

Conclusion

The green building movement is still in its infancy, but it will have an enormous impact in the foreseeable future. Green building is too important a trend to be ignored because it makes sense on so many different levels.

Appraisers' biggest challenge will be to keep up with the changes in technology and new ideas that have not even been considered yet. It is important to keep an open and inquiring mind. The housing industry has undergone rapid changes in recent years and expectations are for even more significant changes in the coming years and decades. New financial products, such as energy-efficient mortgages, are leading the way. The public is becoming increasingly aware of energy efficiency, water and resource conservation, the use of sustainable or recycled products, and measures to improve indoor air quality. Green building addresses all of these issues.

Appraisers need to be on the forefront of these imminent changes. The public looks to appraisers as the experts on housing trends and their impact on values. It will take effort on the part of appraisers, but it is necessary. Appraisers need to undertake independent study to understand green building trends and keep abreast of these changes. The body of knowledge is beginning to grow.

As more and more houses are built or remodeled using green techniques and technology, they will ultimately become the norm. When this becomes the case, non-green houses will experience varying degrees of obsolescence.

It makes sense that sustainable buildings should have more value. They are built better, are better stewards of the environment, consume less energy, and save money on energy costs. They will probably have longer economic lives and provide healthier places for people to live as well as social benefits in the form of less soil and water pollution and fewer carbon emissions.

It is our job as appraisers to measure and quantify these benefits. We should consider ourselves lucky to be appraisers in the midst of these positive changes. The following list provides examples of how appraisers can keep up to date as sustainable practices grow and evolve:

- Take more seminars, such as *An Introduction to Valuing Commercial Green Buildings*, offered through the Appraisal Institute. (Visit www.appraisalinstitute.org/education/ for more information.)
- Visit the USGBC Web site, www.usgbc.org, periodically and read about the latest developments.
- Subscribe to a green building magazine, such as *High Performing Buildings*.
- Go to a trade show, such as the Annual USGBC GreenBuild International Conference and Expo. (Visit www.greenbuildexpo.org for more information.)
- Talk with your local builders about green homes.
- See if your local NAHB chapter sponsors programs related to green building. (Visit www.nahb.org for more information.)
- Earn a green designation, such as the LEED Accredited Professional (LEED AP) or the newly created LEED Green Associate, which may be more relevant for appraisers. (Visit www.usgbc.org for more information.)

Finally, be diligent in your research and data analysis. As appraisers, we need to be in the forefront of the sustainability movement. We will be needed more than ever for our expertise in this changing marketplace.

APPENDIX A

Green Building Online Resources

Organizations

- Alliance to Save Energy (ASE): http://ase.org
- American Society of Heating, Refrigerating and Air-Conditioning Engineers (ASHRAE): www.ashrae.org
- BuildingGreen, LLC: www.buildinggreen.com
- Council of Multiple Listing Services: www.councilofmls.com
- Green Building Finance Consortium: www.greenbuildingfc.com
- Green Resource Energy and Environment Network (GREEN): http://www.boma.org/Resources/TheGREEN/Pages/default.aspx
- National Association of Homebuilders (NAHB): www.nahb.org
- NAHB Green: www.nahbgreen.org
- REGREEN Residential Remodeling Program: www.regreenprogram.org
- Small Wind Certification Council: www.smallwindcertification.org
- U.S. Department of Energy: www.energy.gov
- U.S. Environmental Protection Agency (EPA): www.epa.gov
- U.S. Green Building Council (USGBC): www.usgbc.org

Local Organizations

- Local NAHB Green-affiliated programs: www.nahbgreen.org/WhoIsGreen/hba_findprogram.aspx

Built Green Organizations

- Built Green Colorado: www.builtgreen.org
- Built Green Santa Barbara: www.builtgreensb.org
- Central Washington Built Green Association: www.builtgreencw.org
- Seattle Area Built Green: www.builtgreen.net

Certification/Rating Programs/Standards

- Energy Star: www.energystar.gov
- Green Building Certification Institute: www.gbci.org
- International Code Council (ICC): www.iccsafe.org
- Leadership in Energy and Environmental Design (LEED): www.usgbc.org/leed
- Minimum Efficiency Reporting Value (MERV) Ratings: www.furnacefiltercare.com/merv-ratings.php
- Mortgage Industry National Home Energy Rating Standards: http://www.natresnet.org/standards/mortgage/default.htm
- NAHB National Green Building Standard: www.nahbrc.org/technical/standards/greenbuilding.aspx
- Residential Energy Services Network (RESNET): www.natresnet.org

Products

Daylighting

- Daylighting Collaborative: www.daylighting.org

Deck Products

- Trex: www.trex.com

Geothermal Heat Pumps

- Geothermal Heat Pump Consortium: www.geoexchange.org

Product Certification

- Green Seal: www.greenseal.org

Product Directory

- GreenSpec Directory: www.buildinggreen.com

Radiant Roof Barriers

- Radiant barrier attic fact sheet: www.ornl.gov/sci/roofs+walls/radiant/rb_04.html

Suppliers

- Green Building Supply: www.greenbuildingsupply.com
- Oikos: www.oikos.com
- Ebuild: www.ebuild.com
- Ecohaus: www.ecohaus.com
- Good to Be Green: www.goodtobegreen.com
- Green Building Pages: www.greenbuildingpages.com
- USGBC's Green Home Guide: www.greenhomeguide.com

Remodeling

- Green Home Guide: www.greenhomeguide.com
- NAHB Remodelers: www.nahb.org/category.aspx?sectionID=712
- REGREEN Residential Remodeling Guidelines: www.regreenprogram.org

Publications

- ASHRAE publications: www.ashrae.org/publications
- *High Performing Buildings* magazine: www.hpbmagazine.org
- *The Journal of Sustainable Real Estate*: www.costar.com/josre

Conferences

- Greenbuild International Conference and Expo: www.greenbuildexpo.org
- NAHB National Green Building Conference: www.nahb.org

Reports

- Building Design and Construction's White Papers on Sustainability: www.bdcnetwork.com
- Green Building by the Numbers: www.usgbc.org/News/USGBCInTheNewsDetails.aspx?ID=3923

Case Studies

- 1327 W. Magnolia, Colorado's first LEED-rated "silver" home: www.1327magnolia.com
- Concord, Massachusetts, Retrofit House (from *High Performing Buildings* magazine): http://www.hpbmagazine.org/back-issues/35-back-issues/63-a-home-for-the-next-100-years

- Energy Performance in Residential Green Developments: A Florida Case Study (from *Real Estate Issues* journal): www.cre.org/publications/33_3.pdf#page=77
- Solar Harvest, a "zero net energy" home: www.ecofuturesbuilding.com/2010/03/tour-solar-harvest

Miscellaneous Topics

Geodesic Domes

- Buckminster Fuller Institute: www.bfi.org

Graywater

- Graywater Information Central: www.graywater.net

Green Roofs

- GreenRoofs.com: www.greenroofs.com
- Green Roofs for Healthy Cities: www.greenroofs.org

Incentives

- Database of State Incentives for Renewables and Efficiency: www.dsireusa.org

Invasive Species

- National Invasive Species Information Center: www.invasivespeciesinfo.gov

Multiple Listing Service

- The Green Multiple Listing Service Tool Kit: www.greenthemls.org

APPENDIX B

Guide to Green Building Acronyms

AIA	American Institute of Architects
ASHRAE	American Society of Heating, Refrigerating and Air-Conditioning Engineers
ASID	American Society of Interior Designers
BIPV	building integrated photovoltaics
BREEAM	Building Research Establishment's Environmental Assessment Method (United Kingdom)
CFL	compact fluorescent light
DOE	U.S. Department of Energy
DSIRE	Database of State Incentives for Renewables and Efficiency
EEM	energy-efficient mortgage
EPA	U.S. Environmental Protection Agency
ERV	energy-recovery ventilator
FHFA	Federal Housing Finance Agency
FSC	Forest Stewardship Council
GHG	greenhouse gas
GRHC	Green Roofs for Healthy Cities
HBA	Homebuilders Association
HERS	Home Energy Rating System
HRV	heat-recovery ventilator
ICC	International Code Council
ICF	insulating concrete form

IES	Illuminating Engineering Society of North America
IGCC	International Green Construction Code
IRC	International Residential Code
LEED	Leadership in Energy and Environmental Design
LEED AP	LEED Accredited Professional
LEED AP + Homes	LEED Accredited Professional with Homes specialty
LEED ND	LEED Neighborhood Development
MBA	Master Builders Association
MERV	minimum efficiency reporting value
NAHB	National Association of Home Builders
NREL	National Renewable Energy Laboratory
OFEE	Office of the Federal Environmental Executive
PV	photovoltaic
RESNET	Residential Energy Services Network
SBIC	Sustainable Buildings Industry Council
SERI	Solar Energy Research Institute
SIP	structural insulated panel
SRI	solar reflective index
USGBC	U.S. Green Building Council
VOC	volatile organic compound
WCED	World Commission on Environment and Development

APPENDIX C

Energy Star Thermal Bypass Inspection Checklist

The following checklist has been reprinted from the Energy Star Web site, www.energystar.gov. This checklist must be completed by a certified Home Energy Rater in order for a home to be qualified as an Energy Star home. To complete this checklist, the rater performs a comprehensive visual inspection of building details where thermal bypass–the movement of heat around or through insulation–frequently occurs due to missing air barriers or gaps between the air barrier and insulation. The checklist can be completed electronically or in hard copy. Up to six items on this checklist may be verified by the builder in order to minimize the number of required trips by the rater.

A Spanish version of this checklist and a guide to using the checklist (available as a PowerPoint presentation or PDF file) are also available at www.energystar.gov. Information accessed April 2010. Direct link: http://www.energystar.gov/index.cfm?c=bldrs_lenders_raters.thermal_bypass_checklist/.

ENERGY STAR Qualified Homes
Thermal Bypass Inspection Checklist

The Thermal Bypass Inspection Checklist must be completed for homes to earn the ENERGY STAR label. The Checklist requires visual inspection of framing areas where air barriers are commonly missed and inspection of insulation to ensure proper alignment with air barriers, thus serving as an extra check that the air and thermal barriers are continuous and complete. State, local, and regional codes, as well as regional ENERGY STAR program requirements, supersede the items specified in this Checklist.

Guidance on Completing the Thermal Bypass Inspection Checklist:

1. Accredited HERS Providers and certified home energy raters shall use their experience and discretion in verifying that each Inspection Checklist item is installed per the inspection guidelines (e.g., identifying minor defects that the Provider or rater deems acceptable versus identifying major defects that undermine the intent of the Checklist item).

2. Alternative methods of meeting the Checklist requirements may be used in completing the Checklist, if the Provider deems them to be equivalent, or more stringent, than the Inspection Checklist guidelines.

3. In the event an item on the Checklist cannot be verified by the rater, the home cannot be qualified as ENERGY STAR, unless the builder assumes responsibility for verifying that the item has met the requirements of the Checklist. This option is available at the discretion of the Provider or rater but may not be used to verify more than six (6) items on the Inspection Checklist. This responsibility will be formally acknowledged by the builder signing-off on the Checklist for the item(s) that they verified. The column titled "N/A" should be used when the checklist item is not present in the home or when local code requirements take precedent.

4. The Checklist may be completed for a batch of homes using a RESNET-approved sampling protocol when qualifying homes as ENERGY STAR. For example, if the approved sampling protocol requires rating one in seven homes, then the Checklist will be completed for the one home which was rated.

5. In the event that a Provider or rater finds an item that is inconsistent with the Checklist Inspection guidelines, the home cannot be qualified as ENERGY STAR until the item is corrected in a manner that meets the ENERGY STAR requirements. If correction of the item is not possible, the home cannot earn the ENERGY STAR label.

6. The Provider or rater is required to keep a hard copy record of the completed and signed Checklist. The signature of a builder employee is also required if the builder verified compliance with any item on the Checklist.

7. For purposes of this Checklist, an air barrier is defined as any solid material that blocks air flow between a conditioned space and an unconditioned space, including necessary sealing to block excessive air flow at edges and seams. Additional information on proper air sealing of thermal bypasses can be found on the Building America Web site (www.eere.energy.gov/buildings/building_america) and in the EEBA Builder's Guides (www.eeba.org). These references include guidance on identifying and sealing air barriers, as well as details on many of the items included in the Checklist.

ENERGY STAR Qualified Homes
Thermal Bypass Inspection Checklist

Home Address:______________________ City:______________ State:______

Thermal Bypass	Inspection Guidelines	Corrections Needed	Builder Verified	Rater Verified	N/A
1. Overall Air Barrier and Thermal Barrier Alignment	**Requirements:** Insulation shall be installed in full contact with sealed interior and exterior air barrier except for alternate to interior air barrier under item no. 2 *(Walls Adjoining Exterior Walls or Unconditioned Spaces)*				
	All Climate Zones:				
	1.1 Overall Alignment Throughout Home	☐	☐	☐	☐
	1.2 Garage Band Joist Air Barrier (at bays adjoining conditioned space)	☐	☐	☐	☐
	1.3 Attic Eave Baffles Where Vents/Leakage Exist	☐	☐	☐	☐
	Only at Climate Zones 4 and Higher:				
	1.4 Slab-edge Insulation (A maximum of 25% of the slab edge may be uninsulated in Climate Zones 4 and 5.)	☐	☐	☐	☐
	Best Practices Encouraged, Not Req'd.:				
	1.5 Air Barrier At All Band Joists (Climate Zones 4 and higher)	☐	☐	☐	☐
	1.6 Minimize Thermal Bridging (e.g., OVE framing, SIPs, ICFs)	☐	☐	☐	☐
2. Walls Adjoining Exterior Walls or Unconditioned Spaces	**Requirements:** • Fully insulated wall aligned with air barrier at both interior and exterior, **OR** • Alternate for **Climate Zones 1 thru 3**, sealed exterior air barrier aligned with RESNET Grade 1 insulation fully supported • Continuous top and bottom plates or sealed blocking				
	2.1 Wall Behind Shower/Tub	☐	☐	☐	☐
	2.2 Wall Behind Fireplace	☐	☐	☐	☐
	2.3 Insulated Attic Slopes/Walls	☐	☐	☐	☐
	2.4 Attic Knee Walls	☐	☐	☐	☐
	2.5 Skylight Shaft Walls	☐	☐	☐	☐
	2.6 Wall Adjoining Porch Roof	☐	☐	☐	☐
	2.7 Staircase Walls	☐	☐	☐	☐
	2.8 Double Walls	☐	☐	☐	☐
3. Floors between Conditioned and Exterior Spaces	**Requirements:** • Air barrier is installed at any exposed fibrous insulation edges • Insulation is installed to maintain permanent contact with sub-floor above including necessary supports (e.g., staves for blankets, netting for blown-in) • Blanket insulation is verified to have no gaps, voids or compression. • Blown-in insulation is verified to have proper density with firm packing				
	3.1 Insulated Floor Above Garage	☐	☐	☐	☐
	3.2 Cantilevered Floor	☐	☐	☐	☐
4. Shafts	**Requirements:** Openings to unconditioned space are fully sealed with solid blocking or flashing and any remaining gaps are sealed with caulk or foam (provide fire-rated collars and caulking where required)				
	4.1 Duct Shaft	☐	☐	☐	☐
	4.2 Piping Shaft/Penetrations	☐	☐	☐	☐
	4.3 Flue Shaft	☐	☐	☐	☐
5. Attic/ Ceiling Interface	**Requirements:** • All attic penetrations and dropped ceilings include a full interior air barrier aligned with insulation with any gaps fully sealed with caulk, foam or tape • Movable insulation fits snugly in opening and air barrier is fully gasketed				
	5.1 Attic Access Panel (fully gasketed and insulated)	☐	☐	☐	☐
	5.2 Attic Drop-down Stair (fully gasketed and insulated)	☐	☐	☐	☐
	5.3 Dropped Ceiling/Soffit (full air barrier aligned with insulation)	☐	☐	☐	☐
	5.4 Recessed Lighting Fixtures (ICAT labeled and sealed to drywall)	☐	☐	☐	☐
	5.5 Whole-house Fan (insulated cover gasketed to the opening)	☐	☐	☐	☐
6. Common Walls Between Dwelling Units	**Requirements:** Gap between drywall shaft wall (i.e., common wall) and the structural framing between units is fully sealed at all exterior boundary conditions				
	6.1 Common Wall Between Dwelling Units	☐	☐	☐	☐

Home Energy Rating Provider: ______________ Rater Inspection Date: __________ Builder Inspection Date: __________

Home Energy Rater Company Name: ______________ Builder Company Name: ______________

Home Energy Rater Signature: ______________ Builder Employee Signature: ______________

APPENDIX D

LEED for Homes Checklist

The following checklist has been reprinted from the January 2008 edition of the U.S. Green Building Council's *LEED for Homes Rating System.* This checklist is to be filled out by the builder, engineer, architect, or other responsible party for the property undergoing LEED certification. This form attests to the completion of individual measures and compliance with the requirements for LEED certification.

The *LEED for Homes Rating System* is available at www.usgbc.org. Information accessed April 2010. Note that updates to the rating system are made on an ongoing basis. Direct link: http://www.usgbc.org/ShowFile.aspx?DocumentID=3638/.

LEED for Homes Checklist

Builder Name:
Project Team Leader (if different):
Home Address (Street/City/State):

Project Description:

Building Type: | Project type: |

\# of Bedrooms: *0* | Floor Area: *0.0*

Adjusted Certification Thresholds

Certified:	*45.0*	Gold:	*75.0*
Silver:	*60.0*	Platinum:	*90.0*

Project Point Total: 0	ID: 0	SS: 0	EA: 0	EQ: 0
Certification Level: Not Certified	LL: 0	WE: 0	MR: 0	AE: 0

Notes:
1. *Detailed information on measures below are provided in the LEED for Homes Rating System*
2. *Indicates measures that must be documented using the Accountability Form* (marked ✎)

Innovation and Design Process (ID) (No Minimum Points Required)				Max Points Available	Y / Pts	No	Maybe
1. Integrated Project Planning	1.1	Preliminary Rating		Prerequisite			
	1.2	Integrated Project Team		1			
	1.3	Professional Credentialed with Respect to LEED for Homes		1			
	1.4	Design Charrette		1			
	1.5	Building Orientation for Solar Design		1			
2. Durability Management Process	2.1	Durability Planning		Prerequisite			
	2.2	Durability Management		Prerequisite			
	2.3	Third-Party Durability Management Verification		3			
3.Innovative or Regional Design	✎ 3.1	Innovation #1 ____		1			
	✎ 3.2	Innovation #2 ____		1			
	✎ 3.3	Innovation #3 ____		1			
	✎ 3.4	Innovation #4		1			
			Sub-Total for ID Category:	*11*	*0*		

Location and Linkages (LL) (No Minimum Points Required)			OR	Max Points Available	Y / Pts	No	Maybe
1. LEED ND	1	LEED for Neighborhood Development	**LL2-6**	10			
2. Site Selection	✎ 2	Site Selection		2			
3. Preferred Locations	3.1	Edge Development		1			
	3.2	Infill	**LL 3.1**	2			
	3.3	Previously Developed		1			
4. Infrastructure	4	Existing Infrastructure		1			
5. Community Resources	5.1	Basic Community Resources		1			
	5.2	Extensive Community Resources	**LL 5.1, 5.3**	2			
	5.3	Outstanding Community Resources	**LL 5.1, 5.2**	3			
6. Access to Open Space	6	Access to Open Space		1			
			Sub-Total for LL Category:	*10*	*0*		

Sustainable Sites (SS) (Minimum of 5 SS Points Required)			OR	Max Points Available	Y / Pts	No	Maybe
1. Site Stewardship	1.1	Erosion		Prerequisite			
	1.2	Minimize Disturbed Area of Site		1			
2. Landscaping	✎ 2.1	No Invasive Plants		Prerequisite			
	✎ 2.2	Basic Landscape Design	**SS 2.5**	2			
	✎ 2.3	Limit Conventional Turf	**SS 2.5**	3			
	✎ 2.4	Drought Tolerant Plants	**SS 2.5**	2			
	✎ 2.5	Reduce Overall Irrigation Demand by at Least 20%		6			
3. Local Heat Island Effects	✎ 3	Reduce Local Heat Island Effects		1			
4. Surface Water Management	✎ 4.1	Permeable Lot		4			
	4.2	Permanent Erosion Controls		1			
	4.3	Management of Run-off from Roof		2			
5. Nontoxic Pest Control	5	Pest Control Alternatives		2			
6. Compact Development	6.1	Moderate Density		2			
	6.2	High Density	**SS 6.1, 6.3**	3			
	6.3	Very High Density	**SS 6.1, 6.2**	4			
			Sub-Total for SS Category:	*22*	*0*		

LEED for Homes
Project Checklist (continued)

				Max Points Available	Project Points		
Water Efficiency (WE) (Minimum of 3 WE Points Required)			OR		Y / Pts	No	Maybe
1. Water Reuse	1.1	Rainwater Harvesting System	**WE 1.3**	4			
	1.2	Graywater Reuse System	**WE 1.3**	1			
	1.3	Use of Municipal Recycled Water System		3			
2. Irrigation System	2.1	High Efficiency Irrigation System	**WE 2.3**	3			
	2.2	Third Party Inspection	**WE 2.3**	1			
	2.3	Reduce Overall Irrigation Demand by at Least 45%		4			
3. Indoor Water Use	3.1	High-Efficiency Fixtures and Fittings		3			
	3.2	Very High Efficiency Fixtures and Fittings		6			
			Sub-Total for WE Category:	***15***	***0***		
Energy and Atmosphere (EA) (Minimum of 0 EA Points Required)			OR		Y / Pts	No	Maybe
1. Optimize Energy Performance	1.1	Performance of ENERGY STAR for Homes		Prerequisite			
	1.2	Exceptional Energy Performance		34			
7. Water Heating	7.1	Efficient Hot Water Distribution		2			
	7.2	Pipe Insulation		1			
11. Residential Refrigerant Management	11.1	Refrigerant Charge Test		Prerequisite			
	11.2	Appropriate HVAC Refrigerants		1			
			Sub-Total for EA Category:	***38***	***0***		
Materials and Resources (MR) (Minimum of 2 MR Points Required)			OR		Y / Pts	No	Maybe
1. Material-Efficient Framing	1.1	Framing Order Waste Factor Limit		Prerequisite			
	1.2	Detailed Framing Documents	**MR 1.5**	1			
	1.3	Detailed Cut List and Lumber Order	**MR 1.5**	1			
	1.4	Framing Efficiencies	**MR 1.5**	3			
	1.5	Off-site Fabrication		4			
2. Environmentally Preferable Products	2.1	FSC Certified Tropical Wood		Prerequisite			
	2.2	Environmentally Preferable Products		8			
3. Waste Management	3.1	Construction Waste Management Planning		Prerequisite			
	3.2	Construction Waste Reduction		3			
			Sub-Total for MR Category:	***16***	***0***		
Indoor Environmental Quality (EQ) (Minimum of 6 EQ Points Required)			OR		Y / Pts	No	Maybe
1. ENERGY STAR with IAP	1	ENERGY STAR with Indoor Air Package		13			
2. Combustion Venting	2.1	Basic Combustion Venting Measures	**EQ 1**	Prerequisite			
	2.2	Enhanced Combustion Venting Measures	**EQ 1**	2			
3. Moisture Control	3	Moisture Load Control	**EQ 1**	1			
4. Outdoor Air Ventilatior	4.1	Basic Outdoor Air Ventilation	**EQ 1**	Prerequisite			
	4.2	Enhanced Outdoor Air Ventilation		2			
	4.3	Third-Party Performance Testing	**EQ 1**	1			
5. Local Exhaust	5.1	Basic Local Exhaust	**EQ 1**	Prerequisite			
	5.2	Enhanced Local Exhaust		1			
	5.3	Third-Party Performance Testing		1			
6. Distribution of Space Heating and Cooling	6.1	Room-by-Room Load Calculations	**EQ 1**	Prerequisite			
	6.2	Return Air Flow / Room by Room Controls	**EQ 1**	1			
	6.3	Third-Party Performance Test / Multiple Zones	**EQ 1**	2			
7. Air Filtering	7.1	Good Filters	**EQ 1**	Prerequisite			
	7.2	Better Filters		1			
	7.3	Best Filters	**EQ 7.2**	2			
8. Contaminant Control	8.1	Indoor Contaminant Control during Construction	**EQ 1**	1			
	8.2	Indoor Contaminant Control		2			
	8.3	Preoccupancy Flush	**EQ 1**	1			
9. Radon Protection	9.1	Radon-Resistant Construction in High-Risk Areas	**EQ 1**	Prerequisite			
	9.2	Radon-Resistant Construction in Moderate-Risk Areas	**EQ 1**	1			
10. Garage Pollutant Protection	10.1	No HVAC in Garage	**EQ 1**	Prerequisite			
	10.2	Minimize Pollutants from Garage	**EQ 1**	2			
	10.3	Exhaust Fan in Garage	**EQ 1**	1			
	10.4	Detached Garage or No Garage	**EQ 1, 10.2, 10.3**	3			
			Sub-Total for EQ Category:	***21***	***0***		
Awareness and Education (AE) (Minimum of 0 AE Points Required)					Y / Pts	No	Maybe
1. Education of the Homeowner or Tenant	1.1	Basic Operations Training		Prerequisite			
	1.2	Enhanced Training		1			
	1.3	Public Awareness		1			
2. Education of Building Manager	2	Education of Building Manager		1			
			Sub-Total for AE Category:	***3***	***0***		
			LEED for Homes Point Totals: (Certification level)	***136***	***0*** *Not Certified*		

Project Checklist, Addendum A

Prescriptive Approach for Energy and Atmosphere (EA) Credits

Points cannot be earned in both the Prescriptive (below) and the Performance Approach (pg 2) of the EA section.

Energy and Atmosphere (EA)		(No Minimum Points Required)	OR	Max Points Available	Project Points Y / Pts	No	Maybe
2. Insulation	2.1	Basic Insulation		Prerequisite			
	2.2	Enhanced Insulation		2			
3. Air Infiltration	3.1	Reduced Envelope Leakage		Prerequisite			
	3.2	Greatly Reduced Envelope Leakage		2			
	3.3	Minimal Envelope Leakage	EA 3.2	3			
4. Windows	4.1	Good Windows		Prerequisite			
	4.2	Enhanced Windows		2			
	4.3	Exceptional Windows	EA 4.2	3			
5. Heating and Cooling Distribution System	5.1	Reduced Distribution Losses		Prerequisite			
	5.2	Greatly Reduced Distribution Losses		2			
	5.3	Minimal Distribution Losses	EA 5.2	3			
6. Space Heating and Cooling Equipment	6.1	Good HVAC Design and Installation		Prerequisite			
	6.2	High-Efficiency HVAC		2			
	6.3	Very High Efficiency HVAC	EA 6.2	4			
7. Water Heating	7.1	Efficient Hot Water Distribution		2			
	7.2	Pipe Insulation		1			
	7.3	Efficient Domestic Hot Water Equipment		3			
8. Lighting	8.1	ENERGY STAR Lights		Prerequisite			
	8.2	Improved Lighting		2			
	8.3	Advanced Lighting Package	EA 8.2	3			
9. Appliances	9.1	High-Efficiency Appliances		2			
	9.2	Water-Efficient Clothes Washer		1			
10. Renewable Energy	10	Renewable Energy System		10			
11. Residential Refrigerant Management	11.1	Refrigerant Charge Test		Prerequisite			
	11.2	Appropriate HVAC Refrigerants		1			
			Sub-Total for EA Category:	*38*	*0*		

By affixing my signature below, the undersigned does hereby declare and affirm to the USGBC that the LEED for Homes requirements, as specified in the LEED for Homes Rating System, have been met for the indicated credits and will, if audited, provide the necessary supporting documents.

Project Team Leader		Company	
Signature		Date	

By affixing my signature below, the undersigned does hereby declare and affirm to the USGBC that the required inspections and performance testing for the LEED for Homes requirements, as specified in the LEED for Homes Rating System, have been completed, and will provide the project documentation file, if requested.

Rater's Name		Company	
Signature		Date	

By affixing my signature below, the undersigned does hereby declare and affirm to the USGBC that the required inspections and performance testing for the LEED for Homes requirements, as specified in the LEED for Homes Rating System, have been completed, and will provide the project documentation file, if requested.

Provider's Name		Company	
Signature		Date	

APPENDIX E

U.S. Green Building Council Project Profiles

The following green home project profiles have been reprinted courtesy of the U.S. Green Building Council (USGBC). These profiles exemplify a variety of sustainable, high-performance features in different types of residential properties in different areas of the country. These and many other green building project profiles can be accessed at the USGBC's Web site, www.usgbc.org. From the home page, click on "Resources" and then "Project Profiles," or go directly to the following link: http://www.usgbc.org/DisplayPage.aspx?CMSPageID=1721/.

Five projects are profiled on the following pages:

1. Tepeyac Haven, an affordable housing project in Pasco, Washington
2. The 2008 *Southern Living* Idea House, a detached home in Leicester, North Carolina
3. The Morrisania Homes, an affordable housing project in the Bronx, New York
4. REAL Building's model home, a detached house in St. Petersburg, Florida
5. The Pleasant Hill Home, a detached house in Freeport, Maine

PROJECT PROFILE

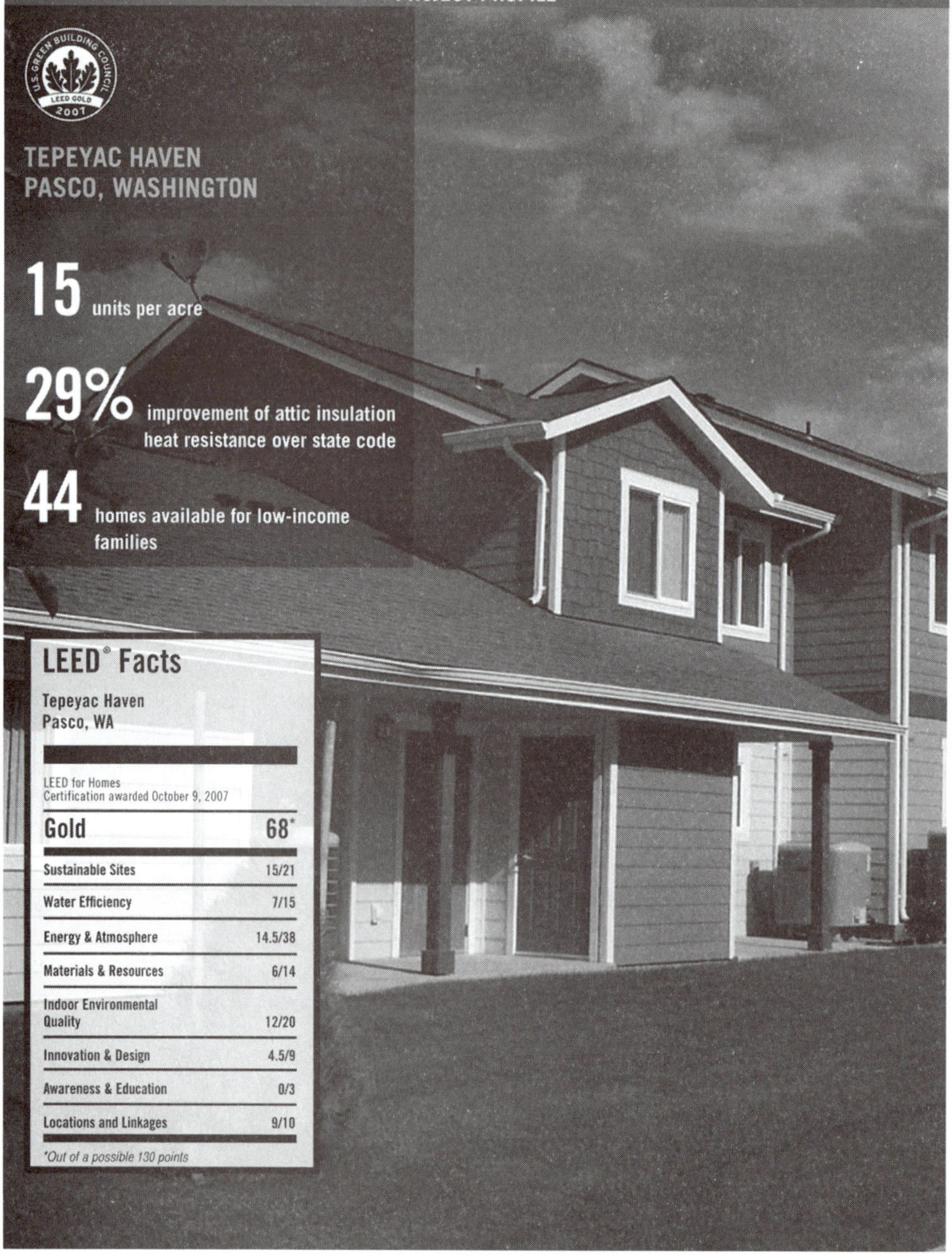

TEPEYAC HAVEN
PASCO, WASHINGTON

15 units per acre

29% improvement of attic insulation heat resistance over state code

44 homes available for low-income families

LEED® Facts

Tepeyac Haven
Pasco, WA

LEED for Homes
Certification awarded October 9, 2007

Gold	68*
Sustainable Sites	15/21
Water Efficiency	7/15
Energy & Atmosphere	14.5/38
Materials & Resources	6/14
Indoor Environmental Quality	12/20
Innovation & Design	4.5/9
Awareness & Education	0/3
Locations and Linkages	9/10

Out of a possible 130 points

PROJECT PROFILE

TEPEYAC HAVEN IN PASCO, WASHINGTON

Affordability Now and Into the Future

Tepeyac Haven's rents are low, and LEED ensures its utility bills will be, too

PROJECT BACKGROUND

When Pasco Family Housing, a project of Catholic Charities Spokane, set out to build its 44-unit affordable housing complex in Pasco, Wash., the organization had more than low rents in mind. For the two-, three- and four-bedroom homes to really benefit their residents, affordability would have to extend beyond the cost of housing and make a dent in the cost of living. Using the principles of LEED®, Pasco Family Housing found many ways to do that by building homes that will cost less to live in for years to come.

"Affordability was never a question," Catholic Charities Spokane executive director Dr. Robert J. McCann said. "The emphasis on energy efficiency during design and construction is directly intended to reduce resident and project operating expenses. In this way, the affordability of the project is beyond just rent levels and considers the total costs to the residents."

"In terms of site selection, the project could not be better – near schools, play fields, shopping and a transit center."

Dr. Robert J. McCann
executive director,
Catholic Charities Spokane

COMING HOME AFTER A LONG DAY'S WORK

Tepeyac Haven is intended for low-income workers in the farms and factories of southeastern Washington's Tri-Cities area of Pasco, Kennewick and Richland. A Tepeyac home comes stocked with a dishwasher, clothes-washer and dryer – all energy and water efficient – and the community includes playgrounds for the kids and easy walking access to everything from schools and play fields to shopping and a transit center. The homes were built on an infill site, making use of existing roads, utilities and other infrastructure. And innovative design methods kept the units small and the density high while maintaining livability.

The high density – 15 units per acre – reduces Tepeyac's literal footprint while also helping cut down its ecological footprint. The community's design leaves lawn areas relatively small, so less water is used. Water use is further reined in by the use of low-flow fixtures and a front-load ENERGY STAR® clothes-washer, aimed at dramatically cutting water bills for homes created specifically with large families in mind.

Architect: Zeck Butler Architects
Contractor: M.C. Lundgren
Engineering Consultants: Storhaug Engineering, L&S Engineering Associates
Development Manager: Beacon Development Group
Project Size: 53,101 square feet
Total Project Cost: $7,300,000 (built with federal affordability tax credits)
Construction cost per square foot: $96.52

STRATEGIES AND RESULTS

In addition to the energy-efficient appliances, energy savings are also achieved through a number of strategies aimed at avoiding wasted energy through air leaks and poor insulation. Ventilation, ducting and air movements were carefully tested to ensure maximum efficiency. Builders used foamed-in-place insulation, resulting in an extremely tight building envelope. And attic insulation has a heat-flow resistance (R factor) of R-49, 29% better than the Washington State Energy Code requires.

Materials used for the home were carefully selected to be durable, healthy and environmentally friendly. Many building materials came from local sources, reducing the pollution and energy use that would have been required to ship the materials from farther away. Painters used low-VOC (volatile organic compounds) products, ensuring residents breathe safe air free of harmful chemicals and toxins. And Tepeyac Haven's use of LEED Accredited Professionals ensured that everyone involved in the design and building process was capable of making the smartest, greenest, most inexpensive choices available.

ABOUT CATHOLIC CHARITIES SPOKANE

Catholic Charities Spokane is the largest sectarian social service organization between Seattle and Minneapolis, providing service to people of all religious faiths in the 13 counties of Eastern Washington. Catholic Charities administers 15 programs that provide food, shelter, clothing, education, counseling and support to those in need, regardless of creed. They include Childbirth & Parenting Alone (CAPA), Counseling, Housing, the St. Anne's Children and Family Center, the St. Margaret's Shelter and Senior Services.

ABOUT LEED

The LEED® Green Building Rating System™ is the national benchmark for the design, construction, and operations of high-performance green buildings. Visit the U.S. Green Building Council's web site at www.usgbc.org to learn more about how you can make LEED work for you.

Printed on 100% post consumer recycled, process chlorine-free paper with non-toxic soy inks.

www.usgbc.org
202 828-7422

Photography appears courtesy of Sheila Gates-Ping, Zeck Butler Architects, PS.

USGBC PROJECT PROFILE

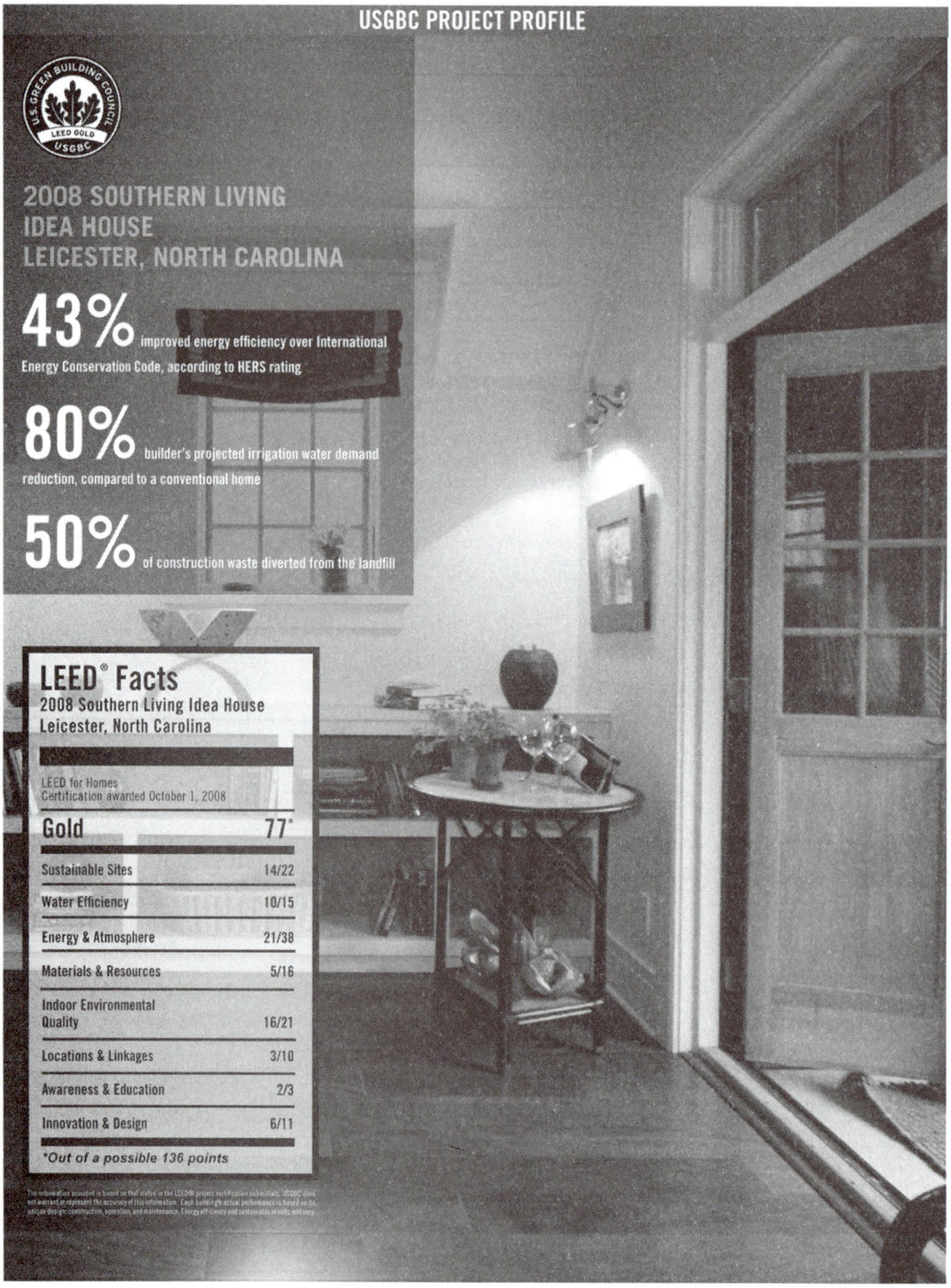

2008 SOUTHERN LIVING
IDEA HOUSE
LEICESTER, NORTH CAROLINA

43% improved energy efficiency over International Energy Conservation Code, according to HERS rating

80% builder's projected irrigation water demand reduction, compared to a conventional home

50% of construction waste diverted from the landfill

LEED® Facts

2008 Southern Living Idea House
Leicester, North Carolina

LEED for Homes
Certification awarded October 1, 2008

Gold	77*
Sustainable Sites	14/22
Water Efficiency	10/15
Energy & Atmosphere	21/38
Materials & Resources	5/16
Indoor Environmental Quality	16/21
Locations & Linkages	3/10
Awareness & Education	2/3
Innovation & Design	6/11

**Out of a possible 136 points*

2008 *SOUTHERN LIVING* IDEA HOUSE

Green Living: A Great Idea

Idea House spreads the word on healthy, green homes

PROJECT BACKGROUND

Southern Living magazine's yearly Idea House feature aims to inspire readers with ideas that can only be spurred by "touring" an innovative house inside and out. It's no surprise, then, that the 2008 Idea House in the Whisper Mountain development near Asheville, N.C., was built with LEED certification in mind. "This house proves that responsible planning and comfortable, achievable living can work hand in hand," the magazine wrote in its profile of the home.

SEEING IS BELIEVING

The Davidson Gap home is a 3,085-square-foot, three-bedroom dream home in the 450-acre Whisper Mountain gated community. Featured in the August 2008 issue of Southern Living, the farmhouse-style home with complementary outbuildings – including a detached garage, cistern "pump house" and more – showcased to millions of people the benefits of a green home and how to achieve one. In addition to the 16-20 million readers who saw the home profiled in the magazine and online, more than 15,000 physically toured the home when it opened to the public. And experiencing firsthand the comfort, durability and style that are possible in a green home is a great encouragement to work toward a green home of your own.

STRATEGIES AND RESULTS

The Idea House was built by EcoBuilders Inc. with a holistic, integrated approach, which was crucial to ensuring all the building and design professionals were on the same page with the home's green features. And those green features are numerous. The home's site was protected from erosion during construction with straw bales, and hardscaping features and swales were designed to prevent erosion into the future. The lot has a minimal amount of impervious surfaces to reduce water runoff. A yard planted with 100% native species, no invasive species, limited conventional turf and drought-tolerant landscaping will cut irrigation water demand by some 80%, the builder estimates. The carriage house's "living roof" aims to cut rain runoff and provide insulation, while a rainwater catchment system provides water to water-efficient dual-flush toilets inside the house.

The home has several features aimed at reducing the amount of energy used and getting as much of that energy as possible from more sustainable sources. A solar water-heating system is backed up by a high-efficiency tankless water heater. This system also acts as the home's primary space-heating source. A super-tight envelope supported by agri-based open-cell foam insulation throughout the house and 2-inch rigid foam under the basement slab help maintain the home's indoor temperature even as the weather changes outside. A zoned heating and cooling system allows residents to maintain a comfortable temperature in rooms where they spend their time but avoid wasting heating and cooling energy in empty parts of the house. And the home is stocked with ENERGY STAR®-rated appliances and lighting. A solar photovoltaic array produces electricity that is sold directly to the local power company.

Special framing techniques helped builders use less lumber while preserving the home's structural integrity. The walls were panelized offsite in a factory, reducing waste, ensuring quality and maximizing space for insulation. And indoor air quality is protected by the use of low-volatile organic compound (VOC) paints and finishes and an energy recovery ventilator that introduces measured, HEPA-filtered fresh air mechanically. And the detached carriage house keeps vehicle pollutants distant from the house.

ABOUT THE *SOUTHERN LIVING* IDEA HOUSE

Southern Living creates its Idea Houses to inspire readers. It strives to show readers homes that look as if the owners have just stepped out. Each year, it features three houses that offer unique ideas, smart design tricks and comfortable interiors.

"Between 16 and 20 million *Southern Living* readers will see this project. Some 15,000-plus people will tour the home. A portion of those people will learn about LEED for the first time or expand their understanding about LEED. The homeowners will live in a home that is healthier for them, with reduced utilities, that is more durable, and will have a lesser impact on the environment as compared to a conventionally built home."
Rob Moody, president, EcoBuilders

Builder: The EcoBuilders
Developer: Whisper Mountain, Ltd.
Architecture: Allison Ramsey Architects, Inc.
Interior Design: Traci Kearns, Alchemy Design
Landscape Design: LaQuatra Bonci Associates
LEED for Homes provider: Southface Energy Institute

Project Size: 3,085 square feet
Buildings: 2
Bedrooms: 3
Photography Courtesy of: Rob Moody

ABOUT LEED

The LEED® Green Building Rating System™ is the national benchmark for the design, construction, and operations of high-performance green buildings. Visit the U.S. Green Building Council's Web site at www.usgbc.org to learn more about LEED and green building.

www.usgbc.org
1-800-795-1747

Photography appears courtesy of Deltec Homes.

PROJECT PROFILE

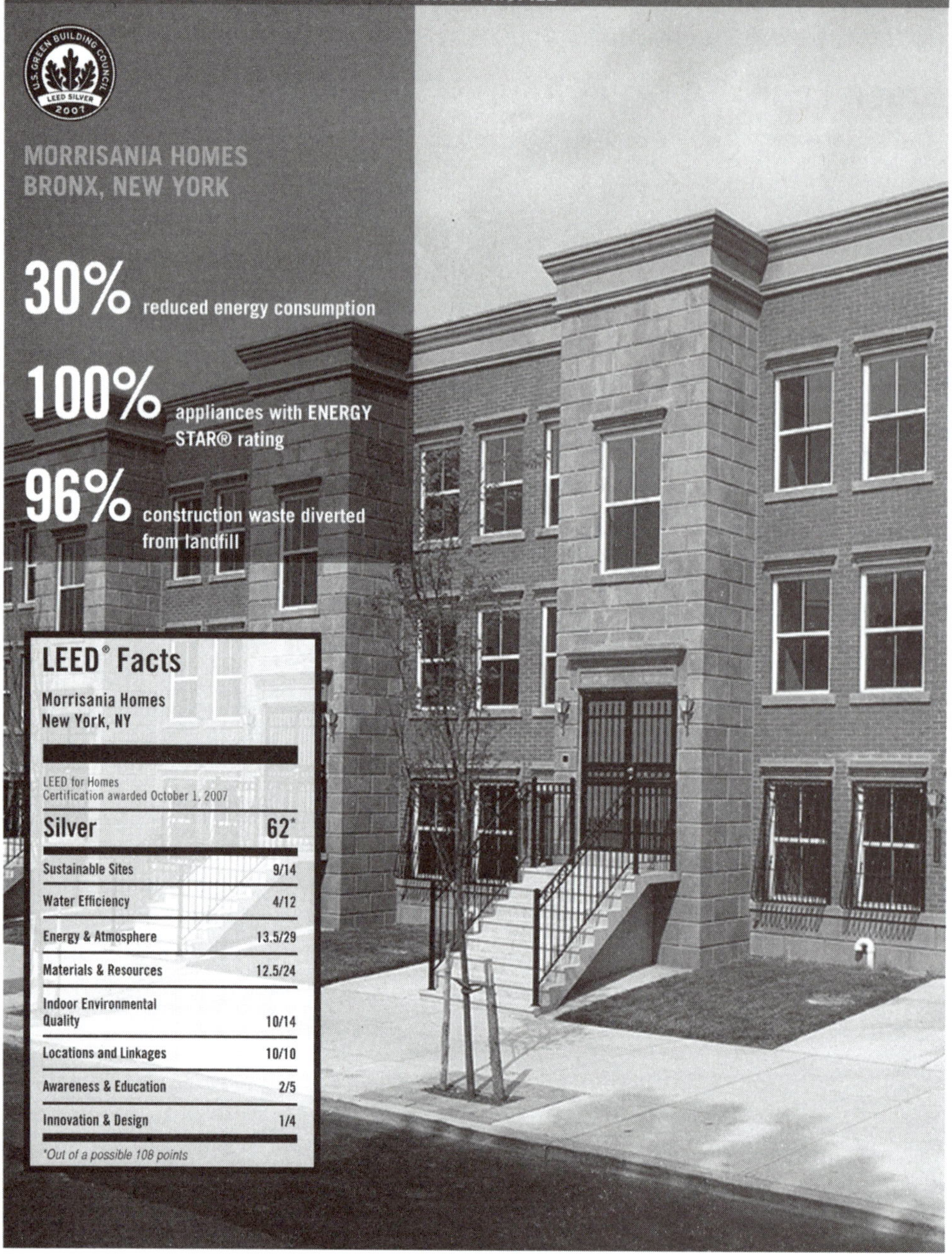

U.S. GREEN BUILDING COUNCIL LEED SILVER 2007

MORRISANIA HOMES BRONX, NEW YORK

30% reduced energy consumption

100% appliances with ENERGY STAR® rating

96% construction waste diverted from landfill

LEED® Facts

Morrisania Homes
New York, NY

LEED for Homes
Certification awarded October 1, 2007

Silver	62*
Sustainable Sites	9/14
Water Efficiency	4/12
Energy & Atmosphere	13.5/29
Materials & Resources	12.5/24
Indoor Environmental Quality	10/14
Locations and Linkages	10/10
Awareness & Education	2/5
Innovation & Design	1/4

Out of a possible 108 points

PROJECT PROFILE

MORRISANIA HOMES IN BRONX, NEW YORK

Affordability Meets Sustainability

PROJECT BACKGROUND

When New York City and state officials began plans for a new affordable-housing project in the South Bronx, they knew they wanted it to offer not just a place to live – but a place to thrive. The resulting Morrisania Homes is just that: an innovative new living environment with a strong focus on protecting the health of its residents and of the surrounding environment.

"This successful development proves that we can have it both ways – we can increase the number of affordable homes, which is essential for working New Yorkers to achieve economic security, and we can do so in a way that also protects the environment and increases energy efficiency," said Gov. Eliot Spitzer. "Green buildings represent a new frontier in the development of sustainable, affordable housing and will help lay the groundwork for a cleaner, healthier and more affordable future."

A JOINT EFFORT FOR THE COMMON GOOD

Morrisania Homes is the state of New York's first affordable-housing project to achieve LEED® for Homes certification. Funding for the project came from a partnership among the state, the city and private investors – a truly collaborative effort that shows how attention to detail can make a big difference in a home's livability and its sustainability. Built by Blue Sea Development with the help of architecture and engineering research and consulting firm Steven Winter Associates, the 28-building, 76-unit mix of two- and three-family homes garners most of its greenness from its smart selection of building materials, fixtures and appliances.

"As we work to build housing for the million new people expected to come to New York by 2030, we need to ensure that we are building homes that people can afford and that allow the city to grow in an environmentally responsible way," Mayor Michael Bloomberg said.

STRATEGIES AND RESULTS

All the homes are stocked with 100 percent ENERGY STAR® rated appliances, as well as efficient sealed-combustion boilers, lighting fixtures and recyclable carpeting. Blue Sea Development has been building all-ENERGY STAR homes for six years, so adding the LEED component seemed a natural next step. The 30% decrease in energy use will save the project's residents big on utility costs.

Morrisania Homes also is equipped with dual-flush toilets, 2-gallon-per-minute shower heads and 1.5-gallon-per-minute sink faucets to dramatically cut back on the homes' water use. The lack of fireplaces and garages, along with continuous background ventilation, keep the air healthy, as does the use of low-VOC (volatile organic compound) paints, cabinet finishes, sealants and adhesives. The builders made use of recycled crushed concrete and masonry and bought locally manufactured materials when possible to reduce the carbon emissions from transporting them.

ABOUT BLUE SEA DEVELOPMENT

Blue Sea Development, LLC, with its principals' combined experience of more than 50 years, specializes in the development and construction of marke-rate, government-assisted, and planned residential developments incorporating sustainable design and construction elements in all their work. Among its recent accomplishments, Blue Sea Development was the first company to build ENERGY STAR and LEED for Homes housing developments in New York state.

"This successful development proves that we can have it both ways – we can increase the number of affordable homes, which is essential for working New Yorkers to achieve economic security, and we can do so in a way that also protects the environment and increases energy efficiency."

New York Gov. Eliot Spitzer

Builder: Blue Sea Development Company
LEED for Homes Provider: Steven Winter Associates
Project Size: 107,792 square feet
Project Cost: $10,457,774

ABOUT LEED

The LEED® Green Building Rating System™ is the national benchmark for the design, construction, and operations of high-performance green buildings. Visit the U.S. Green Building Council's web site at www.usgbc.org to learn more about how you can make LEED work for you.

www.usgbc.org
202 828-7422

Photography appears courtesy of Bernstein Associates/Blue Sea Development Company.

USGBC PROJECT PROFILE
U.S. GREEN BUILDING COUNCIL
LEED GOLD
USGBC
REAL MODEL HOME
ST. PETERSBURG, FLORIDA
46% improved energy efficiency over International Energy Conservation Code, according to HERS rating
30-40% builder's projected indoor water use reduction, compared to a conventional home
25% of construction waste diverted from the landfill
LEED® Facts
REAL Model Home
St. Petersburg, Florida
LEED for Homes
Certification awarded January 22, 2008
Gold 80*
Sustainable Sites 13/21
Water Efficiency 11/15
Energy & Atmosphere 23/38
Materials & Resources 11/14
Indoor Environmental Quality 10/20
Locations & Linkages 6/10
Awareness & Education 2/3
Innovation & Design 4/9
*Out of a possible 130 points

PROJECT PROFILE

PLEASANT HILL (PANISH RESIDENCE)

Building a Dream, While Building Green

PROJECT BACKGROUND

For Mort and Evelyn Panish, building their dream house was synonymous with building a green house. They turned to Taggart Construction, a builder with a longstanding reputation for high-performance, high-quality homes, to help them build a new home on a hilltop location in Freeport, Maine. Their LEED Silver rated, 2,250-square-foot custom home is beautiful, healthy, and good for the environment—and it saves them money.

REWARDING EXCELLENCE

LEED for Homes certification was a natural fit for Taggart Construction. LEED® is a comprehensive framework for the integrated design approach that is the key to high-performance building, and also offers the builder recognition and validation. As Peter Taggart explains, "Some of the most important details of green construction will never be seen. LEED certification recognizes the value in those choices and rewards you for making them." LEED certification gives both homebuilder and homeowner confidence that the home is built to the highest standards, will perform as expected, and is healthy for people and the environment.

STRATEGIES AND RESULTS

Using LEED as a guide from the outset enabled the team to develop the environmental and performance goals in concert with the Panishes' desire for modern amenities, comfort, and universal access and future adaptability. LEED also helped the team take advantage of natural opportunities to lessen environmental impact and maximize performance. For example, the home was located on a reclaimed sand pit to limit the impact zone and excavation. Taggart also maintained existing vegetation and trees; landscaped with native grasses and plants to minimize water use; and installed a stormwater management system to control erosion and protect surrounding fields and forests.

The home's directional orientation maximizes solar gain while helping to power the 3 kilowatt photovoltaic array on the roof. The roof overhangs let in sun during the winter and keep out the high summer sun. Low-E, argon-filled windows are installed throughout the house, and windows on the south side allow sunlight to enter the space in winter, storing radiant heat in the thick tile floor. Additional energy-saving features include compact fluorescent bulbs; high-efficiency appliances; and a propane boiler that delivers hot water on demand. Taggart also used advanced framing techniques and achieved an insulation value of R-27, more than twice the R-value of a typical home. As a result, the Panishes' home is cool in the summer and warm throughout the long Maine winters, while their bills have gone down. "We've been here for one winter, and our heating bills were a third of what most people pay to heat a house this size," Mort Panish says.

To create a healthy and comfortable indoor environment, windows were strategically placed to fill the home with natural light. The home meets the ENERGY STAR® Indoor Air Package standards, providing cleaner, healthier air and protection against airborne pollutants, and even the garage has an automatic exhaust system.

Taggart Construction also sorted construction waste products at every stage of building for recycling and reuse. A large percentage of the construction and building materials have high recycled content, or were locally harvested and milled to reduce shipping costs and fuel use and to support local businesses.

ABOUT TAGGART CONSTRUCTION

Established in Freeport, Maine in 1994, Taggart Construction pursues sustainable approaches to new residential construction, new and historic renovations, additions, and commercial projects. The company's staff of 25 is trained in the latest green building techniques, design practices, materials use, and technologies.

"Living in a LEED home is the best of both worlds. We're doing the right thing for the environment, and we still get to live in the home we've always wanted."

Mort Panish
Homeowner

Owner: Mort and Evelyn Panish
Architectural Designer: Curt Jensch, Taggart Construction
Mechanical Engineer: Pat Coon at Energy Works
Contractor: Peter Taggart
LEED for Homes Provider representative: Danuta Drozdwicz, Fore Solutions
Landscape Designer: Curt Jensch, Taggart Construction
Project size: 2,250 square feet
Project cost: $625,000

Photography courtesy of Peter W. Taggart

ABOUT LEED

The LEED® Green Building Rating System™ is the national benchmark for the design, construction, and operations of high-performance green buildings. Visit the U.S. Green Building Council's Web site at www.usgbc.org to learn more about how you can make LEED work for you.

www.usgbc.org
202 828-7422

Photography appears courtesy of Taggart Construction.

PROJECT PROFILE

PLEASANT HILL HOME
FREEPORT, MAINE

45% more energy efficient

66% lower heating bills

Exceptional indoor air quality

LEED® Facts

Pleasant Hill Home
Freeport, ME

LEED for Homes
Certification awarded May 12, 2006

Silver	**51***
Sustainable Sites	10.5/14
Water Efficiency	1/12
Indoor Environmental Quality	10/14
Materials & Resources	5.5/24
Locations and Linkages	3/10
Energy & Atmosphere	15.5/29
Homeowner Awareness	1/1
Innovation & Design	4/4

**Out of a possible 108 points*

USGBC PROJECT PROFILE

REAL MODEL HOME

Green Living in the Sunshine State

REAL Building's model home is built to withstand all kinds of weather

PROJECT BACKGROUND

When St. Petersburg-based green building consultants REAL Building set out to design and build Florida's first LEED Gold home, their goal was to show that a home of any style could be truly green. The REAL model home in northeast St. Petersburg's Riviera Bay neighborhood is a 2,100-square-foot "Florida-style" home built to blend in with other homes in the nearby community.

A GREEN HOUSE WHERE ANYONE CAN FEEL AT HOME

Darren Brinkley, the founder and president of REAL Building, wanted the home to dispel the myth that a green home is "a mud hut with a chimney in the middle." The model home is designed to be open and welcoming, maximizing natural light while minimizing passive solar heating in the warm Florida climate. It allows for natural ventilation and steady airflow, reducing the need for air conditioning and heating. Its dark flooring is made of rapidly renewable bamboo, which shines in the afternoon light.

The home was built on the site of a rundown 744-square-foot home. Rather than demolishing the old home and discarding it as waste, Brinkley converted it into a two-car garage for the new home. Brinkley deconstructed the old house, recycling much of what he pulled out of it. He estimates that he, his father and a few friends did about 95% of the work deconstructing the old house themselves. The new home was built on pilings above the original home.

STRATEGIES AND RESULTS

The green features throughout the home include light-colored siding to reduce heat gain and minimize the urban heat-island effect; highly efficient Green Seal-certified windows; and striking recycled glass countertops, which serve as the kitchen's centerpiece. Composite decking around the house gives occupants a comfortable place to relax and enjoy the yard's landscaping, which is made up of plants native to Florida.

Structurally, the goal was to build the house to withstand extreme weather, with the main support pillars anchored to reinforced concrete foundations. The house is built using structurally insulated panels (SIPs), a foam-wood composite that creates a tightly sealed building envelope, making the home efficient and strong. The insulation under the main house is a soy-based spray insulation.

In addition to LEED certification, the REAL model home is also an ENERGY STAR®-rated home. The home includes many carefully selected appliances, products and fixtures aimed at improving water and energy efficiency, including compact fluorescent lighting throughout, high-efficiency ceiling fans, ENERGY STAR®-rated appliances, a geothermal HVAC (heating, ventilation and air conditioning) system, dual-flush toilets, a graywater system that uses bath and laundry water to flush toilets, and a 1,000-gallon rainwater cistern for irrigation.

ABOUT REAL BUILDING

REAL is an acronym meaning "responsible, efficient, attainable and livable." REAL Building was founded in January 2006 and strives to build more environmentally friendly homes, limiting the impact on the environment and utilizing green materials that are not only sustainable, but also superior in strength and durability, improving the overall performance of the home.

"Our mission is to create healthy, safe, low-maintenance homes that are responsible, efficient, attainable and livable."

Darren Brinkley, REAL Building founder and president

Design and Consultation: REAL Building
Project Leader: Darren Brinkley
Provider: Florida Solar Energy Center
LEED Consultant: Taylor Ralph

Project Size: 2,100 square feet
Bedrooms: 4
Bathrooms: 3
Cost per square foot: $170
Photography Courtesy of: REAL Building

ABOUT LEED

The LEED® Green Building Rating System™ is the national benchmark for the design, construction, and operations of high-performance green buildings. Visit the U.S. Green Building Council's Web site at www.usgbc.org to learn more about LEED and green building.

www.usgbc.org
1-800-795-1747

Photography appears courtesy of REAL Building. A Design/Build firm offering Green Custom Homes and Renovations.